Silver Spoon Diaries—

Family Memories

Charles King Markline, Sr.

The English language expression "silver spoon" is synonymous with wealth, especially inherited wealth; someone born into a wealthy family is said to have "been born with a silver spoon in their mouth."'

Fulton Books, Inc.
Meadville, PA

Published by Fulton Books 2021

ISBN 978-1-64654-737-1 (paperback)
ISBN 978-1-64654-738-8 (digital)

Printed in the United States of America

Contents

Foreword...5
List of Pictures 7

Chapter 1:   Introduction..11
Chapter 2:   Immediate Family Members that I Remember
                    (Growing Up: Birth to 1959) 12
                    Mother..12
                    My Dad...13
                    A Family Story 15
                    Mam Maw and Pop (Mabel C. and Charles G. Sehrt)...16
                    Papa Cooley (Samuel Wadsworth Cooper) 16
                    Aunt Snooky and Uncle Bill......................................17
                    Uncle Ed and Aunt Cecelia Sehrt 18
                    Aunt Lula and Norman Cameron...............................18
                    Grandpap and Grandmother Markline.......................19
                    Uncle Francis Markline 20
                    Uncle Don and Aunt Sally Markline 21
                    Uncle Elmer and Aunt Gladys...................................22
                    Omie and Elsworth Tanner 22
                    Dad Sperry..24
                    The Ricks Family: Aunt Alice, Big Don,
                            Leonard, Nancy, and Donnie 24
Chapter 3:   The Most Unforgettable Relative....................27
Chapter 4:   Places Where I Grew Up 34
                    Apartments..34
                    4412 Sedgwick Road...34
                    2401 Mayfield Avenue—1944–1949/50 35
                    3604 Kimble Road—1950–1954 37

503 Holden Road—1954–1961.....................................37

2222 Eastridge Road—1961–1965 38

Chapter 5: Schools I Attended 39

Montebello Elementary—Baltimore, Maryland..........39

Towson Junior High School (TJHS)—
  Towson, Maryland 40

Towson Senior High School (THS)—Towson,
  Maryland 40

Augusta Military Academy (AMA)—Fort
  Defiance, Virginia 41

University of Maryland—College Park, Maryland.......41

University of North Dakota (UND)—Grand
  Forks, North Dakota (Classes held at
  Minot AFB, North Dakota) 42

United States International University—
  San Diego, California (Classes held at
  Vandenberg AFB)..43

Chapter 6: A Weekend at 2401 and Eastern Avenue 44

Friday...44

Saturday 44

Sunday 46

Chapter 7: Summer Visits to the Markline Farm Near
  Port Deposit, Maryland..................................47

Get This for a "Life Lesson"...48

Chapter 8: 1959—The Year Everything Changed 49

Chapter 9: College/Fraternity Days..54

Chapter 10: Marriage, USAF Career, Kids 57

Chapter 11: Retirement Years..62

Chapter 12: My Favorites...65

Chapter 13: Words of Wisdom—Life Advice..............................67

Attachments 69

Foreword

My heritage comes from:

Johann Jakob (John Jacob) Markline—1808–1890. He came from Schonach (Baden-Wurthemberg) in southwest Germany and emigrated in 1844.

Heinrich (Henry) Sehrt came from Wolfhausen, Germany (Hesse). Hesse is in southwest/central Germany. Henry emigrated in 1881. The Sehrt name is traced back to 1640 (Hans Sehrt).

John George Cooper (Kupper)—1759–1823. He came from Strasbourg (Alsace Lorraine region in southwestern Germany). Alsace Lorraine is on the French and German border. He emigrated in 1751 from Rotterdam and initially settled in Philadelphia.

Michael King (Great-grandmother Margaret King Markline's father) came from Germany. Dates unknown.

Henry and Louisa Baecker (Baker). They came from the Black Forest area in southwest Germany. Henry emigrated in 1852 coming from Bremerhaven to Baltimore.

My ancestors were merchants, farmers, educators, wheel wrights, morticians, etc. Many were well educated. For example, the Sehrts were school principals in Germany, my pop had a Doctor of Law degree and passed the bar, Uncle Ed had a Ph.D. and was the head of Germanic studies at George Washington while speaking and teaching six or seven languages. Uncle Norman Cameron was a school superintendent, my mother and aunt had college degrees, my dad was an MD, and my grandmothers had nursing and teaching degrees. Michael King served in the Union Army during the Civil War while Silas Cooper paid the United States $300 to legally avoid the draft. Since I went to a military school that was founded to educate the Confederate soldiers coming home from the war, you might say that my family was on three sides in the War Between the States: Union, Confederate, and objector.

I did not put this work together overnight. A special thank-you goes to

- my wife, Judy, for giving me encouragement and a big assist in the editing;
- Roldah Cameron for her inputs on the Sehrt, Baker, and Cameron families;
- Martha Hopkins for her inputs on the Markline family;
- Samuel W. Cooper (my Papa Cooley) for his inputs and stories from the Cooper family;
- last, but not least, to all my grandparents, aunts, uncles, and other relatives for their stories and memories.

List of Pictures

Chapter Number and Title	Picture Number	Description
Introduction	N/A	N/A
Immediate Family Members that I Remember	2.0-1	Four Generations 1942
	2.0-2	Dr. Simeon and Betty Markline
	2.0-3	1939 Pea Green Dodge
	2.0-4	Mam Maw's Sewing Chair
	2.0-5	Aunt Snooky and Uncle Bill 1977
	2.0-6	Pop, Aunt Lula, and Uncle Ed
	2.0-7	Four Generations
	2.0-8	Grandmother Markline
	2.0-9	Me and Mary Christmas
	2.0-10	Swimming with Uncle Elsworth
	2.0-11	Stained Glass Window
	2.0-12	Mother and Dad
	2.0-13	Me, Big Don (Pappy), and Donnie
	2.0-14	My Favorite "Aunt" Alice

Chapter Number and Title	Picture Number	Description
The Most Unforgettable Relative	3.0-1	Sehrt Family 1939
Places Where I Grew Up	4.0-1	4412 Sedgwich Road
	4.0-2	1924
	4.0-3	Completed 2401 Mayfield Avenue
	4.0-4	Uncle Pete
	4.0-5	3604 Kimble Road
	4.0-6	503 Holden Road
	4.0-7	Holden Road Family
	4.0-8	2222 Eastridge Road
Schools I Attended	5.0-1	Montebello Elementary
	5.0-2	Towson High School
	5.0-3	1960–61
	5.0-4	1960–61
	5.0-5	University Chapel
	5.0-6	Sigma Chi House
	5.0-7	Judy and I at Graduation
A Weekend at 2401 and Eastern Avenue	6.0-1	Circa 1950
Summer Visits to the Markline Farm Near Port Deposit, Maryland	7.0-1	The Markline Farm Circa 1950
1959—The Year Everything Changed	8.0-1	Hawaii 1958
	8.0-2	Augusta Military Academy
	8.0-3	Virginia Historical Marker

Chapter Number and Title	Picture Number	Description
College Fraternity Days	9.0-1	The EX Creed
	9.0-2	Forty Years After Graduation
Marriage, USAF Career, Kids	10.0-1	Wedding
	10.0-2	Who Would Have Thought?
	10.0-3	Two Redheaded Kids
	10.0-4	Celebration
	10.0-5	Family Photo
	10.0-6	Thanksgiving 2017
Retirement Years—Failed Several Times	11.0-1	Retirement
	11.0-2	Principal
	11.0-3	On the Field
	11.0-4	Bermuda
My Favorites	N/A	N/A
Words of Wisdom—Life Advice	N/A	N/A

CHAPTER 1

Introduction

The Silver Spoon Diaries should prove that I was not really born with a silver spoon in my mouth (maybe a wooden one).

I recently read an article from Ancestry.com. It stated that 40 percent of Americans are not certain from what country their last name comes, and 25 percent do not know from what countries their families came. Additionally, it expressed concern that many Americans are losing touch with their grandparents. For example, about 21 percent do not know which city any of their grandparents were born, 14 percent do not know what any of their grandparents did for work, and just over 20 percent cannot name a single grandparent's parent.

On the other hand, the article did state that 84 percent of the respondents said it was important to know about their heritage. The top five things Americans wanted to know about their grandparents are the following:

1. Stories of when they were young
2. Childhood memories
3. Where their family came from
4. Their heritage
5. Life advice

In the chapters that follow, I discuss individuals, events, and memories of my childhood. These chapters should get a discussion started. It is my hope is that these diaries will become a "living document" that future generations will update.

CHAPTER 2

Immediate Family Members that I Remember (Growing Up: Birth to 1959)

Mother

Mother was the one I was closest to throughout my life. As most mothers do, she always loved me no matter what. She had a traditional, comfortable upbringing. On the other hand, she did have more than her share of tragedies in her life, outliving three husbands. In a rarity for that era, both Mom and her sister, Mary Louise (aka Snooky), had college degrees. However, she always wanted to be a mother first and foremost.

2.0-1. Four generations 1942: Papa Cooley, Me, Mother, and Mam Maw

As my sister, Beth, put it, Mother was an image of the 1950's, a wife and mom, just like *The Donna Reed Show*. She especially enjoyed the summer months as her kids were home and was sad when school started in the fall. She was set in her basic beliefs about life and about how people should act. She always was a worrier; it got worse later in her life, I think. She was very conscientious about taking care of Pop in his later years. She really didn't like to drive. She loved to read and often took her children to the library. She loved everything "Pennsylvania Dutch" and *always* enjoyed riding around Lancaster, Pennsylvania, going to the markets, eating shoofly pie, and other local dishes. She was also *very* fond of Maryland crab dishes such as crab cakes, crab imperial, etc. She liked to travel but hated driving on high, winding roads. She would close her eyes going over the Bay Bridge even though she wasn't driving. Mom loved to watch and listen to pro football. She wasn't fond of going to see the doctor. I guess she was afraid of hearing something she didn't want to hear. Her friends from childhood were always important to her. The worst time of the year for her was the month of November. Mother hated it as too many close relatives/ friends died in this month. She always said, "I wish I could get under the covers the first of November and get up on the first of December." In her "ideal world" she envisioned:

- Chuck living on the East Coast
- Wayne being married
- Beth having children

She lived until ninety-six. Although her death certificate states that she died on December 1, her spirit "visited" me one last time as it was still November, California time. Her "presence" woke me at 11:45 p.m.; so in my mind she, too, died in November.

My Dad

Simeon Van Trump Markline was born in July 11, 1916. He was named "Simeon" after his grandfather. His middle name was Grandmother Markline's maiden name: Van Trump. He was the oldest of three boys; although my theory is that he was the "only" son. Simeon is a biblical name. Simeon, in the Bible, was the man who first recognized Jesus as the Messiah. Grandmother Markline told the story that when he was little and attended his first vacation Bible school, his teacher told him that he had never heard of someone named Simeon. My dad, even then the jokester, said, "Haven't you ever read the Bible?"

He graduated from Jarrettsville High School and received his pre-med degree from Western Maryland College, a private Methodist college. He was the leader of the Western Maryland band, and Mom was the band sponsor. How did he meet my mother? Here is the story. Mom told a friend of hers that she thought Simeon Markline was cute. Her friend managed to get that word back to my dad. One evening Mom walked out of the dining hall, and there was my dad who walked her back to her dormitory. At Western Maryland, in those days, there were two separate dining halls: one for the men and one for the women. He received his medical

2.0-2. Dr. Simeon and Betty Markline circa 1940

degree in 1940 from the University of Maryland. His graduation was held in the Ritchie Coliseum, across Highway 1, from the University Chapel where Judy and I were married some twenty-five years later. He completed his internship at Temple University where Mom had transferred to finish her degree in childhood education.

He set up his practice on West Thirty-Seventh Street in the Hampden area of Baltimore. His nurse and righthand was "Aunt" Alice Ricks who lived down the street from his office. He always referred to her as Suze. He was on staff at Johns Hopkins Hospital. He had developed some health issues. Evidently, he had contracted tuberculosis (TB) while in med school. It was not discovered until he took his physical for the US Army Medical Corps in Pensacola, Florida. In those days, the treatment was a stay in a sanatorium. He was treated at Eudowood Sanitarium in Towson, Maryland. At the end of this treatment, his condition was classified as an arrested case of TB. In 1944 he contracted pneumonia and passed away at home in November of that year. His funeral was the day after Thanksgiving. Not having him in my life robbed me of the love of a parent, a role model, and most importantly, a dad. His passing left a void in my psyche that will never be filled. That's my story, and I am sticking to it.

A Family Story

On the day my dad passed, Grandmother Markline was called early in the morning and told that he would not make it through the day. It was a school day, so she went to teach. She was called again at noon—same response. By the time she got to Baltimore, her oldest son was gone. Uncle Francis said that his parents were just devastated. She later had a large monument installed over his grave in the Vernon Cemetery. She didn't tell mother ahead of time. Cousin John tells the tale of how many times Grandmother would go to the cemetery and just sit in her car for hours on end. Mother and Dad had two cars: a 1939 pea-green Dodge and a 1940 baby-blue Desoto. Grandmother drove the Dodge for years afterward. As she said, "Until one day it just stopped."

2.0-3. 1939 Pea Green Dodge. Grandmother Markline drove the car for years.

Mam Maw and Pop (Mabel C. and Charles G. Sehrt)

I think Mam Maw had more influence on my growing up and forming my "worldview" than anyone else in my life. Mabel Cooper Sehrt's parents were Samuel Wadsworth Cooper and Mary Louise Stine. She grew up in Southern Pennsylvania in the Millersburg/Elizabethville area. She earned a nursing degree. She married Pop in 1916.

They built the house on Mayfield Avenue in 1924. Both of them lived in that house until their deaths. Pop said he never wanted to be in a nursing home. He wanted to be carried out of 2401 "feetfirst." Although Pop was the head of the family, it was Mam Maw who directed the day-to-day activities. Pop always picked up the check when we went out to eat (I have since picked up that mantel).

2.0-4. Mam Maw's sewing chair. It was a wedding present in 1916; I had it redone.

After Mam Maw passed away, Pop remarried around 1963 to Kay Kraft. Kay was a good friend of Pop's sister, Aunt Lula.

I suspect Aunt Lula engineered the introduction at a card party at Aunt Lula's house. Please note: Mam Maw and Aunt Lula were not the best of friends. According to Mother, it was always Mam Maw and Aunt Cecelia on one side and Aunt Lula on the other. My guess is that Aunt Lula was a little bit of a prima donna in her own mind.

Mam Maw and Pop are discussed in more detail in several other chapters.

Papa Cooley (Samuel Wadsworth Cooper)

Samuel Cooper was born in Southern Pennsylvania in Dauphin County and lived in Elizabethville and Millersburg, Pennsylvania areas. He was a licensed civil engineer responsible for the design and layout of Millersville, Pennsylvania. He was married to Mary Louise Stine, who died much earlier than he. I am not sure of when he moved in with Mam Maw and Pop, but he did live at 2401 for quite some time. He read the Bible frequently and got into trouble with the local authorities during one of the blackouts early in World War II for leaving his bedroom lights on so he could read the Bible. I always said, "'Good night, Papa Cooley,'" when Mother put me to bed. He wrote down a record about the history of his family in addition to a couple of his short stories (see attachment entitled *Cooper Chronicles*).

According to Mother, Papa Cooley had a theory on the average length of a cold: "If you have a cold and take medication, the cold will last seven days. If you have a cold and don't take any medication, it will last a week."

Aunt Snooky and Uncle Bill

Aunt Mary Louise (aka Snooky) was Mom's younger sister by five years. How did she get the nickname "Snooky"? The story I heard was that one of the maids called her Snooks when she was a small child, and I guess it just stuck. If you look at family pictures, she looks almost exactly like Papa Cooley's wife, Mary Louise Stine. Everyone has a favorite aunt, and she was mine. I would always receive the best Christmas and birthday presents from Snooky and Bill. She was athletic and could really fire a baseball. She also played a little tennis in her younger days. I think she was closer to Mam Maw than Mom as they talked on the phone almost every day. She graduated from Western Maryland College where she earlier met William (Bill) G. Parks.

After the war, she and Bill were married at the Eutaw Church up the street on Mayfield Avenue. The reception was held at 2401. I remember the wedding. I sat with Mother and Aunt Johnny. Bill was a captain in the US Army in WWII. He was wounded in the shoulder during the New Guinea Campaign and later contracted yellow fever. He was recalled during the Korean

2.0-5. Aunt Snooky and Uncle Bill, 1977. I really miss these guys.

War and was stationed in Vienna, Austria. Snooky joined him there. He was a salesman and a good one for several paper companies—first in Baltimore, and later in Columbus, Ohio. He was, for a long time, my "fill-in" dad. He always played cowboys and Indians with me, and later we spent hours playing baseball. He passed away in 1986. I still miss talking with him. Snooky and Bill adopted two children, Jim and Janet. They were roughly about the same age as Wayne and Beth. Snooky and Bill welcomed Judy into the family with open arms. After Bill's death, Snooky visited us in California a couple of times. She never got over losing Bill so soon after his retirement. I really think her ultimate cause of death was a broken heart.

Uncle Ed and Aunt Cecelia Sehrt

Edward Henry Sehrt was the oldest of five children, with three who reached adulthood: Uncle Ed, Pop, and Aunt Lula. Of all the Sehrts, he is easily the most mentioned on the modern-day Internet. There is a detailed discussion of him in the *Uncle Ed Chronicles*. Aunt Cecelia (née Shane) was Uncle Ed's first wife. Several years after her death, he married one of his students, Helen Ludwig. Uncle Ed and Aunt Cecelia's only child was Little Cecelia. She was Mother's age and along with Mother was a flower girl in Aunt Lula–Norman Cameron wedding. She was severely burned during a Fourth of July celebration and died several days later. She is buried in the Sehrt family plot in Loudon Park Cemetery in Baltimore. Uncle Ed and Aunt Cecelia are also buried in the family plot.

Aunt Lula and Norman Cameron

Aunt Lula (Louise Marguerite) was the youngest of five children of Henry and Caroline Baker Sehrt. She married Norman Cameron on August 11, 1920. Dr. Cameron was a gradu-

2.0-6. Pop, Aunt Lula, and Uncle Ed, 1960

ate of the University of Pennsylvania and a lifelong educator. He was principal of the Baltimore Teachers Training School, the president of State Teachers College at West Chester, Pennsylvania, and later the superintendent of Schools for the Garfield, New Jersey, public-school system. They had two children, Norman Jr. and Caroline.

Norman Jr. and Caroline were well educated. Norman Jr. was a Harvard graduate and served as vice president of one the largest financial credit companies in the United States. Caroline taught many years at Gettysburg College and was married to Tom Henderson. Norman Jr. married Rolda, who was a Vassar graduate. She contributed greatly to the Sehrt and Baker chronicles. Mother told me that one time they were having Christmas dinner at the Cameron's house. Dr. Cameron made young Norman (who was going to Harvard at the time) get up from the dinner table and go to his room to study. Mother also told me that Dr. Cameron would curse the hours he slept during his life when he could have been engaged in further learning activities. He died of a heart attack in 1947 and is buried in the Loudon Park Cemetery.

Grandpap and Grandmother Markline

Francis (Frank) King Markline was the third of five children. He was born in 1890 and passed away in the spring of 1960.

Jessie Mae Van Trump was the oldest child of Simeon James Van Trump (1865–1933). Grandmother always referred to him as Papa, and her mother was Sarah Jennie Trout (1872–1928).

As far as I know, they always resided in the White Hall area of Maryland. At one time, part of that area was called Trump. Aunt Gladys told me that Grandpap could have married any number of single ladies in that area but that he only had eyes for Jessie. Not sure what year they were married, but my dad was born in July 1916. Grandmother, a school teacher, taught the fifth grade at

2.0-7. Four Generations: my dad, Me, great-grandfather Philip, and grandfather Frank Markline

Jarrettsville Elementary for thirty-three years. Grandpap was a US mail carrier working out of the White Hall Post Office. Their house, still standing, is on School House Road in White Hall, overlooking the old railroad bed. In 1947 (I think) they bought a farm just above the town of Port Deposit, Maryland.

2.0-8. Grandmother Markline as I remember her

The farm was 113 acres and looked like it could have been painted by Norman Rockwell. It was real Americana with a large stone house, all the traditional farm out-buildings that were painted red-with-white trim. They paid $28,000 for it! Grandpap continued to deliver mail and lived at the White Hall property during the week and drove over to the farm on weekends. Grandmother and Francis moved over to the farm. Grandmother continued teaching while Francis worked the farm.

I don't know when Grandpap retired, but Grandmother taught at Jarrettsville until she hit mandatory retirement. She then taught at a private school until several weeks before her death. They were polar opposites in many ways: Grandpap was slender, smallish, and seldom held a long conversation with anyone; Grandmother was a big woman for her day, and Uncle Francis said that when she entered a room, she sucked all the oxygen out of the room—quite the conversationalist! Grandmother was also a super cook. I can still see her making dinner rolls from scratch, each one perfectly formed when they went into the oven. Grandpap passed away in 1960, and Grandmother passed in 1968. I miss them both.

Uncle Francis Markline

Francis Phillip Markline was born in 1930 in the house on School House Road in White Hall, Maryland. He was the youngest of the three boys. He was educated at Boy's Latin in Baltimore. He rode the train from White Hall to Baltimore every day. He received a good education and always wrote extremely well. After my grandparents bought the farm, he became a farmer and milked the cows, plowed the fields, planted, and other chores. He did do a tour with the US Army during the Korean War. Ambition was not his forte. He often said, "My goal in life always was to be mediocre, and I succeeded." He taught Cousin Eddie and I how to throw a curve ball during one summer's visit to the farm. He was terrible at managing money.

One year after he lost the farm and moved into a trailer in Rising Sun, Maryland, I sent him $1,000 to pay his heating bill. Uncle Francis told me that my dad once took him to an Oriole baseball game at Old Oriole Park located at Greenmount and Twenty-Ninth Street, a wooden stadium that burned down in the summer of 1944. During the game, one of the players got injured, and the team doctor was not present. The announcer asked if there was a doctor in the house. My dad went on the field and treated the player. As my dad walked off the field, the fans cheered. Francis was very impressed with his oldest brother!

2.0-9. Me and "Mary Christmas." Picture taken on the front yard of the White Hall property.

Uncle Don and Aunt Sally Markline

Donald Dunnick Markline was born in 1919 and was the second of three boys of Frank and Jessie Markline. He attended University of Maryland for a couple of years. He married Sally Gill, who was a good friend of mother when they were sisters-in-law. Uncle Don ran a gas and auto-repair station located with the family home across from the intersection of York and Wiseburg Roads, North of Cockeysville, Maryland. Later he delivered the US mail. A lifelong smoker, he contracted emphysema and died from that disease. Sally and Don had four children: Edward Francis (six months younger than I); Donald Simeon (died in a car crash in 1964); John Elsworth, and Judy Ann. Don and Sally are buried in Timonium, Maryland, along with Simmie in the Delaney Valley Memorial Gardens.

Uncle Elmer and Aunt Gladys

Elmer Philip Markline was the second child and first son of Philip H. Markline and Margaret Ann King Markline. He was born in 1886. Gladys Margaret was the last of five children and was born in 1901. Elmer fought in World War I and was classified as a disabled veteran; although I don't know what his injury was. He looked a lot like Grandpap Markline. It was easy to tell they were brothers. He worked at the funeral home along with my great-grandfather Philip Markline and his brother, Howard Stanley Markline. Aunt Gladys worked as a secretary in Baltimore for years. After the funeral home closed, Elmer went to live with her. I asked Aunt Gladys one time what was the biggest change she observed in her lifetime. She said when she was growing up the funeral home needed to have a phone. She said there were two wind-up phones in their entry hallway: one was connected to the South into Maryland, the other went North into Pennsylvania (Note: White Hall, Maryland is about fifteen miles south of the Mason-Dixon line). Both Elmer and Gladys are buried in the family plot in the Vernon Cemetery in White Hall, Maryland.

Omie and Elsworth Tanner

Naomi Adeline Van Trump Tanner (Omie)—Grandmother Markline's younger sister. She and my Grandmother Markline never got along too well. Omie was an excellent cook and used to make baked beans from scratch. I think she was very close to my dad and was of great help to Mom the last weeks of my dad's life. I remember Omie as an outstanding real estate agent.

Christopher Elsworth Tanner (Uncle Elsworth)—He was a great uncle and husband to Omie. He worked in District Steam for the Baltimore Gas and Electric Company. Several years after Omie's death, he "married out of the

Uncle Elsworth Summer 1944

2.0–10. Swimming with Uncle Elsworth, 1944

22

family" when he married Howard Markline's widow, Asenath Ward Markline.

Omie and Elsworth lived in Baltimore on Graystone Avenue when I was little. They moved to Monkton, Maryland, and later to the Green Spring Valley in Baltimore County. Never having children of their own, they were foster parents to a number of boys and kept in touch with several of them all their lives. My cousin Simeon (Simmie) lived with them. I went on several vacations with Omie, Elsworth, and Simmie: one year to the Great American Corn Festival in Oklahoma, the next year a tour of the West (Yellowstone, Grand Tetons, Bryce Canyon, Zion Canyon, and the Grand Canyon), and the next year to Nova Scotia.

Simmie died in an automobile accident, flipping his new sports car near Loyola College on his way home. He was speeding, and it was his first day of driving his new vehicle that Uncle Elsworth had bought for him. He is buried with his mom and dad in the Delaney Valley Cemetery in Timonium, Maryland. Aunt Omie had to deal with a heart problem most of her adult life. She was a little on the heavyset side, so that didn't help the situation. She passed away in the early 1960s and is buried alongside Elsworth in the West Liberty Church Cemetery, near White Hall, Maryland. Her parents and grandparents are also buried there. In the inside nave of the church is a stained-glass window dedicated to her grandparents, Simeon and Elizabeth A. Van Trump.

*2.0-11. Stained-glass window located on an inside
wall at The West Liberty Methodist Church.*

Dad Sperry

Charles F. Sperry came into my life 1951–52; though I don't know the exact date. Dad Sperry, Mother, and I lived on Kimble Road until 1954 when we moved to 503 Holden Road in Towson, Maryland. Early on he suspected that I was suffering from "academic laziness." He was Mom's third husband. They had known each other when they were growing up. Their marriage brought into my life something new: a brother, Wayne Allen, and a little sister, Beth Ann.

2.0-12. Mother and Dad, Easter 1975

Wayne was born in 1952, and Beth followed about eighteen months later. Dad Sperry was married to mom over forty-plus years. His income from the phone company was such that Mom could be what she always wanted to be—a mother and a housewife. They would travel to Florida frequently to get away from the Maryland winters. I am pretty sure I picked up my love of new cars from him as he was always "wheeling and dealing." Dad Sperry took me to game three of the 1966 baseball World Series. The Orioles won 1-0. I think they had an excellent marriage, and Mom surely deserved this lifelong relationship. They are buried at the Delaney Valley Memorial Gardens not far from their home on Eastridge Road.

The Ricks Family: Aunt Alice, Big Don, Leonard, Nancy, and Donnie

Aunt Alice was not really my biological aunt; she was my dad's nurse, and he always called her Suze. When I was small and visited them, she would go to the little market next door to their house and buy a box of powered donuts. She and I had a good time drinking tea and having several powered donuts. "Big" Don was an electrician with the City of Baltimore. He also worked at Memorial Stadium and was my supplier for used bats and baseballs. Big Don loved his beer and

Camel cigarettes. He taught me how to steam shrimp. He always "flavored" the water with a can of beer.

Leonard was the eldest son from Alice's first marriage and was a member of the Baltimore Fire Department. Nancy was the youngest child and also a nurse. Donnie was a few years older than I and never married. He was a sharp dresser and worked for a men's store called Frank Leonard's. He always lived at home and took excellent care of his parents (bought the house, paid the mortgage and other bills). He died of cancer—too early in life—a lifelong smoker. They lived several years on Thirty-Sixth Street, down the street from my dad's medical office. Big Don, Alice, and Donnie later moved to Towson. When Nancy called me and told me my aunt Alice had passed, I cried for hours. I miss all of them. Even though they were not "blood relatives," they were always very special to me.

Beach 1946

2.0-13. Me, Big Don (Pappy), and Donnie. Mother and I went to Atlantic City with them.

A couple of other things about the Ricks family:

Aunt Alice must have thought my dad was the cat's meow. She told me he was quite the jokester. I think Mom and Dad spent a lot of time with Alice and Big Don. For a while Big Don was unemployed, and my dad picked up their bills. Pappy was one of my dad's pall bearers. Aunt Alice was so distraught at my dad's passing she could not bear to attend his funeral. I often wonder if she ever visited his final resting place?

2.0-14. My favorite "Aunt" Alice. She was one of the nicest people you would ever want to meet.

CHAPTER 3

The Most Unforgettable Relative

"Pop" was quite a character. He is still fondly remembered many years after his passing. I inherited a lot of his characteristics.

My grandfather (Pop), Charles George Sehrt, was born in Baltimore, Maryland, on July 2, 1890. He was the second son of Henry and Louise Sehrt. He was educated at Baltimore City College and received his Doctor of Law degree from the University of Maryland. He married Mabel Elizabeth Cooper in 1916. They had two daughters, my mother, Elizabeth Augusta, and my aunt, Mary Louise. Although he passed the bar exam, he never practiced law. He bought his father's dry-goods-and-hardware business that was located at 3425 Eastern Avenue in a section of Baltimore known as Highlandtown. German immigrants settled Highlandtown, and my great-grandfather, Henry Sehrt, came there from Germany in 1881. My earliest memories of my grandfather were at the family home at 2401 Mayfield Avenue.

3.0-1. Sehrt Family 1939: Mother, Mam Maw, Pop, and Snooky. Note the blanket. This photo was taken November 2, 1939. Most cars did not have heaters installed then.

I remember my grandfather as a sometimes strict but kindly individual, with a twinkle in his eye. He was somewhat tight with his money, but his family was well cared for (for example, we never really wanted for anything, and household servants, such as a maid and gardeners, were always close by). The only exception to his thriftiness was the money spent on his family's education. For example, both my mother and aunt were college educated, which was somewhat unusual for that time.

My grandfather, known to all family members as Pop, was a creature of habit. He always arose and arrived home at the same time, making sure he had dinner at 6:00 p.m. sharp, so he could listen to Lowell Thomas and the news broadcast. As conservative in dress as he was in politics, he seldom left the house without his three-piece suit and fedora. He repeated his weekly activities on a regular basis. One of his activities was setting the clocks every Sunday morning. As a child, I considered it a great adventure to join him on his Sunday-morning rounds, setting the cuckoo clock and the large grandfather clock in the living room. The cuckoo clock now belongs to my cousin, Janet, while the grandfather clock (built in 1814) stood proudly in the corner of my dining room at 1300 Quarter Horse Trail in Santa Maria, California, for many years. It now is in my son's (Charles Jr.) house in Los Angeles, California.

Pop passed away on November 14, 1986. He will always be remembered as quite a jester and kidder, and many of his stories and comments, often corny, are part of the family's history. Here is a sample of some of his most memorable.

Situation	Pop's Comments
For Thanksgiving and other special meals when turkey was being served	"My country "tis of thee, sweet bird of cranberry, I love thy breast and wings, feathers, and other things."
On his response to a knock on the door	"Who is without?"
On education	"Make sure that for every dollar you spend on education that you get one hundred cents out of it."
On Franklin Delano Roosevelt	"Roosevelt ran for president four times, and I never voted for him once."
On Harry S. Truman	"A rascal."
On his response to someone sneezing	"Gesundheit, dunkeshon"
On mother-in-law and marriage	"Do you have a mother-in-law yet? You had better get one. The supply is running short."
The story with no ending	"There were three men out in a boat. They had one oar. That oar had a hole in it. They had a flat tire, and they were three miles from a gasoline station."
On anyone (me included) returning from Sunday school or church	"What did you learn in Sunday school? Did they tell you about Moses amongst the bull rushes?"

Situation	*Pop's Comments*
On his response to the mention of the word "coffee"	"I like coffee. I like tea. I like Shorty (substitute other names, if appropriate), and Shorty likes me."
On his response to the mention of the word "peaches"	"Peaches, peaches, my nose eetches."
The sauerkraut joke	"In old Germany, it was the custom to name the first son by the maiden name of the mother. That was fine until the time came when the father's name was Kraut, and the mother's name was Sauer."
On his comment on any food you didn't like (such as green beans)	"Green beans? They will put hair on your chest."
On his response to the mention of the word "fish"	What kind of fish? Gefiltefish?
On his rejoinder to the question, "What is your teacher's name?"	"Mrs. Applecrumbie?" PS It is believed that Mrs. Applecrumbie was Pop's Sunday-school teacher—not sure about that one.
If your teacher's name was Mrs. Hammond	"Mrs. Hammond, she played the Hammond organ."
On Pop's comment on anyone who walked with a cane or gimped on a sore leg	"He walks like he has a bone in his leg."
On the creation of holy water	"Just take regular tap water, put it in a pot, turn on the stove, and boil the hell out of it."
On one of important events of American history	"In 1492 Shakespeare crossed the Delaware."

Situation	Pop's Comments
On his version of the multiplication tables	"Two times two is twenty-two, three times three is thirty-three"
Pop on poetry	Pop could quote (completely) "The Raven" by Edgar Allen Poe, "The Rubaiyat of Omar Khayyam," and Tennyson's "The Charge of the Light Brigade," as well as "Twas the Night Before Christmas."
On describing a person's (male) physical appearance	He was a short, tall, slim, stout, bald fellow with red curly hair and a black moustache.
On his comments when I returned from seeing a Saturday-afternoon cowboy movie	"Who did you see? Tom Mix 'n Cement?" Note: Tom Mix was one of the original cowboy actors. Mix 'n Cement was a cement mix sold in Pop's hardware store.
Some more poetry from "Casabianca" by Felicia Hemans, 1829, that went like this: "The boy stood on the burning deck Whence all but him had fled; The flame that lit the battle's wreck Shone round him o'er the dead"	Pop's version: "The boy stood on the burning deck His feet were full of blisters He looked aloft, his pants fell off And now he wears his sister's"
On his definition of a "graveyard secret"	Dead from now on
On his explanation of birthdays	Pop used to say that you only had one actual birthday; for all subsequent years it was a birthday anniversary.

Situation	*Pop's Comments*
On his definition of a Tin Roof Cocktail	On the house
On his favorite cheer	"Ricketty, racketty ree, kick 'em in the knee. Ricketty, rackety, ras, kick "em in the other knee"
On mentioning someone taking pills (for any reason)	"What are they taking? Carter's Little Liver Pills?" *Note:* Carter's Little Liver Pills were "toddies for the body" that cured whatever ailment you were suffering from, or imagined you were suffering from. Carter's Little Liver Pills were a patented medicine by Samuel J. Carter, and the active ingredient is bisacodyl. The history of the pills is they were to be used as a laxative-aiding bile flow. They were first put on the market in 1938, and in 1951 the FTC told the company to take out the word "liver" in the title of the product. It was a very popular product that was advertised heavily up until the 1960s and resulted in a popular phrase being used: *"He/she has more than Carter has Little Liver Pills."* The pills were liver-colored and really had nothing to do with your liver.
Whenever I mentioned my great-aunt Omie (actual name Naomi, my grandmother Jessie Markline's younger sister)	Na-oh-my

Situation	*Pop's Comments*
My nickname, no matter how tall I grew	Shorty

CHAPTER 4

Places Where I Grew Up

Apartments

My mom and dad lived in a couple of apartments until 1943. I think at least one of the locations was an apartment owned by Great-aunt Omie and Great-uncle Elsworth Tanner. Mom and Dad rented an apartment on the second floor of the large Tanner home on Gladstone Avenue (I think).

4412 Sedgwick Road

Somewhere around late 1943 or early 1944, Mom and Dad bought this house. It had a white picket fence around it; Mom always mentioned that fact. According to Zillow, the house was built in 1935, 1 1/2 baths, approximately 1,700 sq. ft. It is located near Loyola College in Baltimore off of West Cold Spring Lane. From the picture the master bedroom faced the front of the house (second floor), and the windows (first floor) is where the dining room was. One time when Mother and I drove past the house, she pointed out the second-story window and said, "That is the room where your father

4.0-1. 4412 Sedgwich Road where I lived 1943–44

breathed his last." I only have two faint memories of that house. The first one is the only memory I have of my dad. We were standing at the culvert at the nearby Stony Run Park, and he was holding my hand. I swear that is all I personally remember about him. The second memory of this house was not pleasant. I had said (mind you, I was 2 1/2), "Dammit the hell." Mother sat me down on the dining-room table and put pepper on my tongue. I haven't said "Dammit the hell" since.

2401 Mayfield Avenue—1944–1949/50

The 2401 property was bought by Pop and Mam Maw in 1923 from Judge Dobler (his house is up the street toward Harford Road), and construction was completed 1924.

4.0-2. 2401 Mayfield Avenue under construction, 1924

The house is located at the corner of Mayfield and Norman Avenues and is catty-corner to St. Matthew's Lutheran Church. The house is a two-story with a large basement. The basement had dressing room and bathroom for the maid. There was a separate two-car garage by the alley (to the right in the picture). On the first floor, there was a large formal living room with a never-used fireplace, a tiled sun parlor with a fireplace that backed up to living-room fireplace, large dining room, two bedrooms downstairs, a full bath, and a kitchen with pantry and breakfast nook. On the second floor there was a sunroom at top of the stairs, two large bedrooms, Pop's office and law library, and bathroom with large tub that rested on clawed feet.

4.0-3. Completed 2401 Mayfield Avenue. This picture was taken in the 1940s or 50s.

I was within easy walking distance to Montebello School. It was close enough that I could walk home for lunch that Mam Maw would cook for me. Come to think of it, I never ate cafeteria food at either Montebello, Towson Junior High, or Towson High School; maybe I did have a "silver spoon?" St. Matthew's Church was a High Lutheran Church. It was one of three churches in a two-block area. Reverend Gottlieb Siegenthaler was the minister. Pop always referred to him as the "Holy Father." Pop was not big into church ceremony. To the left of 2401 in this picture lived

4.0-4. Uncle Pete. Uncle Pete used to play with Dick Jarrett and Me.

the Jarrett family consisting of Cliff and Chris Jarrett, Aunt Bea (Cliff's sister, I think), Uncle Pete (Peter Kohlis, Chris's uncle, I think), and son, Dick.

Uncle Pete taught me how to keep score for baseball games and smoked Uncle Willie cigars. Their house probably still smells like stale cigars. Dr. Grossfield's family lived on the other side of 2401. The children were Leonard, Dorothy (my age), and Gregory. Gregory had olive skin, and Pop always call him "the little Mexican." The Pente family lived across the street, as did the Yursicks and "the Pierpont girls" (Pop's phase for the three spinsters that lived next to the Jarretts).

3604 Kimble Road—1950–1954

This house was bought by Mom and second husband, Gordon Hickman Freeman, somewhere around 1949/50. Kimble Road intersects with Thirty-Sixth Street that runs right behind where old Memorial Stadium once stood. It was a two-story house with small basement (the basement had a restroom). On the first floor was a sunroom (front), living room, dining room, and a small kitchen. The

4.0-5. 3604 Kimble Road. 3604 is the center house in this picture.

second floor had three bedrooms and a full bath. The neighbors were the Moores and the Cades. Since we lived so close to the stadium, I was able to park cars in our driveway at five dollars each when the Baltimore Colts were playing (a lot of money in those days). During football season, Memorial Stadium was known as the "largest outdoor insane asylum."

503 Holden Road—1954–1961

Dad Sperry, Mom, Wayne, and I moved out of the city and into Baltimore County. This move was traumatic for me. I missed the city! The house was newly built house when we moved in to this middle-class development. The house was in a new neighborhood and had four bedrooms and two full baths. Dad Sperry did build an enclosed back porch. He did all the work himself as I recall. Since I had just graduated from Montebello, I was able to skip 1/2 year of seventh grade. I started at Towson High in 1955. The school was close enough for me to either walk or ride my English bike (bikes didn't need a lock for the bikes in those days). While at Holden Road, I delivered *The Morning Sun* paper for several years, six days a week.

4.0-6. 503 Holden Road. This picture is the current view as of 2018.   *4.0-7. Holden Road family: Mother, Wayne, me, Dad Sperry, and Beth.*

2222 Eastridge Road—1961–1965

The family moved to Timonium, Maryland, in 1960. Since I was attending the University of Maryland during the early 1960s, I only lived there during the summer and the holidays. It was a single-story house with a large semi-finished basement. I started living alone in 1965. Judy and I married August 28, 1965.

4.0-8. 2222 Eastridge Road. Dad Sperry and Mother bought this house when it was new.

CHAPTER 5

Schools I Attended

Montebello Elementary—Baltimore, Maryland

Montebello School opened in 1924, Mother's first year at the school. The school is located at the intersection of Thirty-Third Street and Harford Road on the shores of Lake Montebello. The school is located approximately five blocks from 2401 Mayfield Avenue. I was there for seven years, kindergarten through sixth grade, graduating in February 1954. When I started, Mother and I were living at the Mayfield Avenue home. During my first year, Mother used to walk me back and forth. Later I would walk to school and back, as well as coming home for lunch. I never ate in the cafeteria. It was an "experimental school." Occasionally we would be excused at 10:00 a.m. and return at 2:00 p.m. for classes where we were observed by other teachers and educators.

5.0-1. Montebello Elementary Mother and I both attended

Towson Junior High School (TJHS)—Towson, Maryland

After a February graduation from Montebello, I tested into the middle of the seventh grade. I only attended TJHS for a year and a half.

Towson Senior High School (THS)—Towson, Maryland

I started THS in the fall of 1955, the newest high school in Baltimore County.

The school is in a white middle-class neighborhood just off York Road. My guess is that the total enrollment was somewhere around 1,500 students. The environment was safe, and the students, for the most part, enjoyed a carefree and peaceful time at the high school. I had a number of friends, but no really close ones. I never dated anyone in my graduating class and really didn't date much until late in my junior year. Being shy at that time, I had almost zero activities. Since we lived fairly close to the school, I walked or rode my English bike to school. I graduated June 5, 1959. THS was the first high school alumni group formed on the East Coast, and currently it has the largest alumni group in the nation.

5.0-2. Towson High School, 69 Cedar Avenue, Towson, Maryland

Augusta Military Academy (AMA)— Fort Defiance, Virginia

I enrolled in AMA in September 1959. This marked the first time I was away from Baltimore for an extended period. I took courses such as physics, Latin III, and others that I had avoided at Towson. For additional information on my time at AMA, see the Chapter 8, *1959—The Year Everything Changed*. I received my post-graduate degree in June 1960.

5.0-3 and 5.0-4. 1960–61, in AMA uniform at school and in front of 503 Holden Road.

University of Maryland— College Park, Maryland

I enrolled in the University of Maryland in September 1960 on my way to cramming 4 years in 5 1/2 years. Originally, I was an education major but changed to business administration during my initial registration. I am a third-generation alumni of the university. Pop had a Doctor of Law degree, and my dad received a medical degree in June 1940 (his graduation ceremony took place in Ritchie Coliseum, which was directly across Highway 1 from the

5.0-5. University Chapel. Judy and I were married here, August 28, 1965

chapel where Judy and I were married a quarter of a century later). I enrolled in Air Force ROTC my first year.

During my stay at Maryland, I lived in campus housing my first two years. My roommate in Charles Hall was Jim Barley who lived in Towson, and his dad bought him a black-and-yellow Ford Fairlane, so we drove home on weekends in style. Later I joined the Sigma Chi Fraternity and lived in the fraternity house. I was able to lose most of my shyness and became involved in several campus activities. In fact, I went from almost zero activities to many. I made Who's Who in American Colleges and Universities, 1964–65 ed. I finally graduated in February 1965 with a Bachelor of Science degree in business administration and was commissioned second lieutenant in the USAF. As a Distinguished ROTC graduate, I came into the USAF as a regular officer.

5.0-6. Sigma Chi House, 4600 Norwich Road

University of North Dakota (UND)—Grand Forks, North Dakota (Classes held at Minot AFB, North Dakota)

I enrolled in UND in early 1970 as part of the Minuteman Education Program. This program was set up for missile combat crew members to earn their MBA degree in conjunction with their crew duties. It did take me a semester to figure out that you needed to maintain a B average at the graduate level. I graduated in 1973. The graduation exercises were held on campus in Grand Forks.

United States International University—San Diego, California (Classes held at Vandenberg AFB)

In 1977, at the start of my second tour at Vandenberg AFB, Dr. Jim Collins got me interested in a Ph.D. program that was being offered at the base. The major was leadership and human behavior. This degree was a mix of business, psychology, and sociology. I used part of my veteran's benefits to offset the program costs. Classes were held on weekends on Vandenberg AFB. To meet residency requirements, I completed several semesters at the San Diego campus on weekends. Since I had an excess of

5.0-7. Judy and I at graduation ceremony held at Grand Forks campus

credits from my MBA program, I was able to graduate a little earlier than normal. The title of my dissertation was "A Comparative Analysis of College Entry Program and High School Initial Students: Study Habits and Attitudes, Sex, Age, GPAS, and Other Selected Variables." Graduation exercises were held in San Diego in June 1980.

CHAPTER 6

A Weekend at 2401 and Eastern Avenue

Friday

In the winter season, if I were at 2401 on a Friday night, we often went to a "Travelogue" presentation at the Lyric Theater. Pop drove, and his neighbors, the Yursicks, would go with us. The Yuricks lived across the street on Mayfield Avenue. If the Yursicks didn't go with us, Bill and Snooky would go with us. We parked at the B&O Station across the street from the Lyric.

Saturday

After lunch on Saturday, Mam Maw and I headed down to the store on Eastern Avenue. The grocery and hardware store were located in a section of Baltimore called Highlandtown, where the Germans originally settled. Upon arrival, I played ball in the back of the house, bouncing my tennis ball off the steps of an outbuilding they called the Granary. The two side-by-side stores were separated by an enclosed alleyway. The stores were on the first floors. The back of the grocery store and the second floors were where the family used to live before moving to Mayfield.

When I was little, the apartment above the hardware store housed the Cooks Dancing Studio. Later Mrs. Flynn, who worked in the grocery store, lived in the apartment. Ed Cole and George Zeller worked in the hardware store; Pop helped there when they got busy. The back and second floor of the grocery store was fully furnished. On the first floor was a living room, a sitting room, a large dining room, and a dated but serviceable kitchen. Located upstairs were several bedrooms and a bathroom with a claw-foot tub. We usually had an early dinner, often beef stew or roast beef with all the fixings. After dinner, I would head down the street to the Grand Theater. Almost always, on Saturdays, it played a Western movie starring either Gene Autry, Roy Rogers, or *The Durango Kid*. After the movie, I would return to the store. Pop would always ask, "How was Tom Mix and Cement?" *Note*: Tom Mix was one of the early Western heroes; Mix "n Cement was a dry concrete mixture that was sold in the hardware store.

6.0-1. The grocery and hardware stores on Eastern Avenue circa 1950

Mam Maw and I would leave the store earlier than Pop who would be ready to close the store. Pop would open the back gate to the property, and Mam Maw would drive back to 2401. When I visited, I slept in the second downstairs bedroom that was connected to the master bedroom via a walk-in closet. I believe the second bedroom was Snooky's old bedroom (not sure). This room had a window A/C unit that I always put to good use during the warm Baltimore summers. Mam Maw would have me say my prayers before I fell asleep.

Sunday

In the morning the three of us would have breakfast: eggs, bacon, toast, fruit, etc. Afterward Pop would take me around the house with him to wind/adjust the clocks and fill the radiator trays with water (winter time). He would then read me the "'funny papers" with stories of the Katzenjammer Kids, Blondie, The Days of Prince Valiant, and The Phantom.

After early Sunday School at St. Matthew's Church, I would go down to the store with Pop. The store had three large tin bins at the front for regular pretzels, hard pretzels, and ginger snaps. While he was checking the stores, I would take a couple of ginger snaps to Fritz, the collie watchdog. Pop and I would go back to 2401 for lunch. After lunch, Pop would take a nap, and Mam Maw and I would to the movies, to the park, or take flowers to the Loudon Park Cemetery that is located off of Wilkens Avenue. In the family cemetery plot rests Henry and his wife, Pop and Mam Maw, Uncle Ed, Cecelia, little Cecelia, Aunt Lula and Uncle Norman, as well as the two children that did not grow into adulthood. Next to the Sehrt plot rests Cousin Harry, Aunt Eva, and Cousin Margaret. Mother used to say that there wasn't much left of Cousin Margaret. Prior to her death, she had a mastectomy and lost a leg to diabetes.

Later in the afternoon, Dad Sperry, Mother, Bill, and Snooky would arrive at 2401 for dinner. I always had a baseball and a couple of gloves waiting for Uncle Bill. He would always play catch with me in the front yard. For dinner we usually had something like roast beef, crab cakes, and crab imperial.

After dinner, everyone went out to the front porch. We would all sit down, have a conversation, and just be family. Everyone was on their way home by 8:30 p.m. Pop had to keep to his schedule of being in bed by 9:00 p.m.

I can always vividly remember every moment of weekends like this. I wish I could live it again—just one more time!

CHAPTER 7

Summer Visits to the Markline Farm Near Port Deposit, Maryland

My grandparents, Frank and Jessie Markline, owned three properties: a house in White Hall on School House Road (Francis was born there, and the picture of me and the pony, Mary Christmas, was taken in front of this house), an apartment in Forest Hills (don't ever think I was there; I think it was a converted old school house), and a 113-acre farm that was located above the town of Port Deposit, Maryland. I think they bought the farm around 1947. Of the 113 acres, 98 were acres on the side of the road where the house was located, and 15 acres were directly across the highway. The farm was complete: stone house, barn, all the outbuildings normally found on a classic American farm, red with white trim; a "Norman Rockwell" setting if there ever was one.

7.0-1. The Markline Farm circa 1950. This is the way I remember it.

I asked Uncle Francis why they ever bought the farm. He said, "Mom always wanted to live in a stone farmhouse." Catch was that this one came with 113 acres! The property was purchased for $28,000! The house was built in three phases: the middle (hard to see in this picture) housing the main kitchen and breakfast area, the back section that occasionally was rented out, the front section had Grandmother's dressing room, dining room, a large living room, and a circular staircase leading to the bedrooms and bathroom. Originally, the farm had an outhouse (ugh). Later indoor plumbing was added. My visits to the farm were significantly different from the 2401 visits. The visits to the farm were measured in weeks instead of days. I usually spent part of my summer at the farm. My cousin, Eddie, often joined me. Eddie was six months younger than I, so we got along splendidly. Mostly the days were filled by helping Uncle Francis with some of his farm chores (a lot of work). Eddie and I probably drove him crazy from time to time. Eddie and I always managed to play baseball every day. Frequently Uncle Francis took Eddie and me into "Port" to see a movie.

Get This for a "Life Lesson"

Just to the left of the driveway was a one-acre garden. Sweet corn, tomatoes, and green beans were grown there. One summer the garden had a lot of weeds growing between the rows. Grandpap, Eddie, and I set out one morning to weed the garden. It was a hot and sticky July day. Being from the city, I quickly got bored with all this manual labor. Grandpap and Eddie made great progress in cleaning out the weeds while I was falling way behind. Soon it was lunchtime. When we sat down to the table, Eddie discovered a five-dollar bill under his plate. On the other hand, I had a one-dollar bill under my plate. Nothing was ever said, but I got the message.

I can vividly remember Grandmother cooking all day during harvest season when a number of other farm workers helped out. Man, she could really cook.

CHAPTER 8

1959—The Year Everything Changed

Growing up in the 1950s was a great experience. Children were brought up to respect their elders, the church, their teachers, etc. The biggest technical advancement, as I recall, was the affordability and availability of television in the home. I lived a carefree existence. However, for me, many changes were on the horizon. These changes came to fruition in 1959. They centered on graduation from high school, going away to prep school, as well as illness and death to close family members. The biggest news in Baltimore at the end of 1958 was the Baltimore Colts were World Champions, having been successful in "The Greatest Football Game Ever Played."

In Baltimore 1959 started off quietly enough. We still lived at 503 Holden Road in Towson, Maryland. Dad Sperry was still working with the telephone company, and Mom was doing what she always wanted to do—be a mother. Sister Beth was five, and Brother Wayne was seven. The home was a four-bedroom; Wayne and I had the upstairs rooms and shared a bathroom and shower. I was a senior at Towson High and enjoyed the idea that I was in the senior class of the roughly 1,500 student body. Although I remember my high school years fondly, I was still shy, lazy academically (a situation that followed me until I got into my Ph.D. program many years later), and I had almost zero school activities. I definitely was not on anyone's "Most Likely to Succeed" listing. On the other hand, I delivered *The Morning Sun* papers and worked part-time in the produce department at Food Fair.

Pop and Mam Maw still lived at 2401 Mayfield Avenue. Pop was five years into retirement, and he and my grandmother had been doing some travelling. In those five years they had been to Europe twice and had a cruise to Hawaii.

8.0-1. Mam Maw and Pop on Vacation, Hawaii 1958

They still hosted weekly Sunday dinners, eating at around 5:30 p.m. and everyone leaving NLT 8:30 p.m. (Pop still had to maintain his schedule). The Sunday-meal participants had grown since my earlier years with the welcome additions of Wayne, Beth, as well as Snooky and Bill's kids, Jimmy and Janet.

Aunt Snooky and Uncle Bill still lived on Rexmere Road. In the next eighteen months they would move to a new home just North of Towson.

On the other side of the family, Grandmother Markline, Grandpap, and Uncle Francis lived at the family farm, located just above Port Deposit, Maryland. Grandmother was still teaching fifth grade at Jarretsville Elementary, Grandpap was retired from the postal service, and Francis worked the farm. Great-uncle Elsworth, Great-aunt Omie, and Simeon lived in the Greenspring Valley of Baltimore County. Aunt Sally, Uncle Don, and kids (Eddie, John, and Judy) continued to live in Parkton, Maryland (I think Don was a postal employee by that time).

At home the big issue was, what was I going to do after graduation? My dad, Mother, Snooky, and Bill had all attended Western Maryland College (now McDaniel) in Westminster, Maryland. Naturally, I had always thought that would be my next academic stop. One minor hiccup—I was not accepted. So, now what?

After much family discussion, two things became clear: one, academically I was not ready for college; two, it seemed like military prep school would be a good option. We looked at several different ones. The most affordable was Augusta Military Academy (AMA—https://amaalumni.org) in the Shenandoah Valley. Only catch was that to make it more affordable, I had to wait tables (ugh, not like the guy who was born with a silver spoon). After week-long activities, I graduated from Towson High School on June 5, 1959. During the summer months, I continued working for Food Fair and delivering the morning papers. In September Dad Sperry, Mother, and I loaded up the Nash station wagon and travelled down the Blue Ridge Mountains into the Shenandoah Valley via Highway 11 to AMA. Upon arriving, Dad Sperry met Colonel Roller and made sure I was enrolled in the tough courses of physics, college algebra, and others. These were the courses that I had avoided at Towson. Later in the day I said goodbye to my family, my childhood, and started on the path of "leaving the nest."

*8.0-2. Augusta Military Academy. This is a picture of
the main barracks after AMA's closure in 1984.*

All "new" cadets were required to "brace on the stoops" and be in formation at first bugle call. As a cadet waiter, I was a member of the Headquarters Company and was able to eat meals first before we waited/cleaned the tables for the rest of the Corps of Cadets.

In October I received a sad letter from Grandmother Markline letting me know that Grandpap had a severe case of oral cancer. Near the middle of November, I was called into Colonel Roller's office and was told that my Grandmother Sehrt had passed away. Naturally, when told, I thought that he was mistaken and that he meant Grandpap. I left AMA at dawn the next day; it was during the Greyhound bus transfer in Richmond that I had, for the first time, noticed what is now called racism in the form of a "whites-only drinking fountain."

Mam Maw's death was unexpected. She was always healthy, but in the summer, she had contracted a terrible ear infection that had to be treated with very powerful drugs. Later we surmised that the drugs had caused a weakening of her heart. She was the center of our family and a more caring person never lived. Snooky always referred to her as an "absolute saint." When she died, part of the close family ties died also. I will never forget the love and attention she freely gave to her oldest grandchild. At AMA there was no Thanksgiving break. At home, due to the recent passing of my grandmother, the celebration of the fourth Thursday of November was very low-key.

The Christmas break at AMA was three weeks long. It was good to be home after four months away. Celebrating this year was a lot different than previous years. The Christmas holiday in 1959 was subdued. No longer would the Christmas dinners be presided over by Mam Maw and Pop at 2401. The fancy Christmas dinners, cooked and presented by Mam Maw and Janey Bell, were now a thing of the past—gone forever. Too soon the holidays were over, and I was back at AMA. The second half on my time at AMA passed quickly. Grandpap Markline passed away in the spring. I graduated from AMA in June 1960. Pop joined Dad Sperry, Mother, Wayne, and Beth to watch the ceremony and a full dress parade. That summer I worked as a teller for one of the banks in Baltimore.

As my life moved from 1959 to the 1960s, it was like a period ending a sentence and a capital starting the next. The changes began to accelerate. In the fall of 1960 I finally started my college career at the

University of Maryland. In late 60/early 61, Snooky and Bill moved from Rexmere Road to the county (Charmuth Road), and we moved from Holden Road to Eastridge Road. Gone were the weekly dinners at 2401 Mayfield Avenue. Gatherings were still held at Thanksgiving and Christmas; only they were in restaurants such as the Blackstone on Thirty-Third Street. The days of old were gone forever, but their memories clearly linger in my mind's eye to this day.

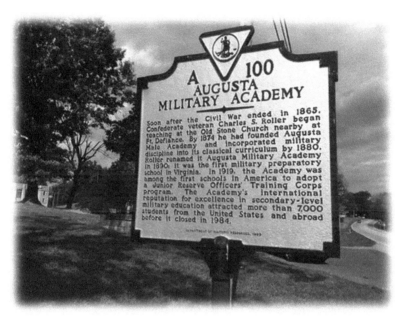

8.0-3. Virginia historical marker; location is on Lee Highway in Fort Defiance, Virginia

CHAPTER 9

College/Fraternity Days

I attended University of Maryland from September 1960 to February 1965, cramming 4 years into 5 1/2. I initially started in the Department of Education. However, I switched to the School of Business during my initial registration in the fall of 1960. I lived on campus the entire time. The first two years I spent in the men's dormitories, ending up in Charles Hall. The remaining time I lived in the Sigma Chi house on Knox Road (later torn down). The fraternity now calls Number 14 Fraternity Row its home.

Initially I lived in the EX house and later pledged, becoming an active brother in 1963.

I made lifelong friends with my fraternity brothers. We made up nicknames for each other: "Peaches" was from Georgia; "Bear" was a burly individual; "Douche Bag" was George Doetsch; "Beetle" and "Seed" were small in stature; "Chief" (short for Chief Firewater) couldn't hold his booze; "Fingers" lifted a whole set of silverware from the campus dining hall for our dinner table; "Notch" had a small notch of skin missing on one ear; "Fish" was an All American diver on the Maryland's Swim Team; and, I was "The Buzzard."

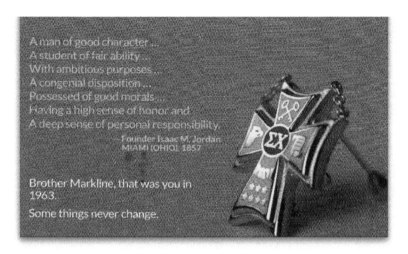

A man of good character ...
A student of fair ability ...
With ambitious purposes ...
A congenial disposition ...
Possessed of good morals ...
Having a high sense of honor and
A deep sense of personal responsibility.
—Founder Isaac M. Jordan
MIAMI (OHIO) 1857

Brother Markline, that was you in 1963.
Some things never change.

9.0-1. The EX creed—I was a good example of the second bullet on this list

We pulled a lot of pranks but never got caught. Once several fraternities got together (EX included) and hatched a plan to steal the Navy goat before a basketball game between Maryland and the Naval Academy. The goat was reported missing, and during the first half of the game, every time Maryland scored a basket, the crowd roared, "Navy, Navy, we got the goat." At halftime the goat was brought on the floor and delivered to the Naval Academy representatives.

Now days we would be kicked out of school, and the fraternity deactivated. What a bunch of woozies we have become. The brothers were always playing games with each other. For example, during the early sixties, Pope John XXIII was on his deathbed. He hung on for days. One of the brothers suggested we set up a "pope pool" (bet on what hour the Pope would pass away).

My roommate, Chief, won the bet. Boy, then the teasing started. A cross was painted on our room door; Chief was referred to as "The Pope Killer," etc. Chief felt so bad he took the money he had won and, under the cover of darkness, put it in the poor box at the local Episcopal church. Years later we started having annual reunions at Emerald Isle, North Carolina. Many of the brothers are still married to their college sweethearts, including me! The stories get better every reunion.

9.0-2. Forty years after graduation; some things never change

CHAPTER 10

Marriage, USAF Career, Kids

I met Judy Woods at the EX Spring Formal in 1964. She was on a blind date with Brother Roger Howell, and we ended up sitting at the same table. I was dating one of her sorority sisters who was also named Judy (not real serious, but attractive). In early June, after final exams, I saw Judy again on the beach in Ocean City.

Well, that did it. I made sure I saw her the next weekend at University of Maryland summer-school registration. I got there when registration opened and waited six hours for her to show up. When the fall semester started, we saw each other almost every day. I must have been a bad influence on her as she said her grades went down after meeting me. Of course, mine stayed about the same. We got engaged later that fall. After Christmas, we drove to Shelby, North Carolina, so I could meet her extended Greer family so they could check me out. Who is the Yankee? I don't think I ever felt more welcomed in all my life! Southern Hospitality! We were married at the University of Maryland chapel, August 28, 1965.

Reverend Harold Wright presided. He was a classmate of my parents at Western Maryland College. He christened me and presided over my dad's funeral in 1944. We lived in a brand-new apartment in Greenbelt, Maryland, $120 a month including utilities. Judy taught English at North Bethesda Junior High School, and I was a ceremonial officer in the USAF Honor Guard at Bolling AFB. That job was the best one I ever had. I spent a lot of time at Arlington National Cemetery doing full honor ceremonies. We moved on base in 1967 while I was a general's aide. In 1969 I volunteered for missile duty and later received orders to Minot AFB, North Dakota.

Before we left DC, Catheryn was born at Andrews AFB on our fourth wedding anniversary. I went to missile training at Chanute AFB, Illinois, and Vandenberg AFB, California. While I was in training, Judy stayed with Nana and Bill in South Laguna Beach, California. I went on alone to Minot until we were assigned base housing. Finally, we were on a "real AFB." Minot had a missile wing, a bomber wing, a tanker squadron, and a fighter squadron. As part of Minuteman III crew duty, I was enrolled in an MBA program concurrent with missile duties. Mark was born April 3, 1971, at the VA Hospital in downtown Minot. We spent four winters in Minot. Snow was often on the ground from Halloween to May. We met folks there that have been our friends ever since. I received orders for Vandenberg AFB in the fall of 1973. We drove to California that December, spent the holidays at South Laguna Beach, and arrived at Vandenberg AFB on January 2, 1974. Initially we lived on the base and in 1976 bought our first home in Vandenberg Village. Judy began teaching at Allan Hancock College.

10.0-1. Wedding reception at Bolling AFB

She was an English instructor for AHC starting in 1975. In 1976 I was selected for promotion to Major and was tabbed for Armed Forces Staff College in Norfolk, Virginia. I went to Norfolk in January 1977, graduating in June. I lucked out and received a return assignment to Vandenberg where I would stay for the rest of my AF career. Judy was well on her way with her own career. During this time, she received her MA degree from Cal Poly, became dean of the Lompoc Center, and later became one of the academic deans on the main campus. She did all this and managed to also help coach the girls' softball team. In 1981 I was promoted to lieutenant colonel. Initially Catheryn and Mark went to public schools in Vandenberg Village. In 1983 we moved to a new house in Mesa Oaks. Judy, Mark, and I took horse riding lessons.

10.0-2. Who would have thought? We haven't changed too much in our fifty years together.

We stabled our horses, Kelly, Popcorn, and April next to the La Purisma Mission. The mission had over nine hundred acres of well-maintained riding trails. Mark was the best rider.

10.0-3. Two redheaded kids Catheryn and Mark

He won the county championship one year in both English and Western. Both Catheryn and Mark attended St. Joseph High School in Santa Maria. In 1987 we moved to Santa Maria (Westrail Estates) and took the horses with us.

Catheryn graduated from St. Joseph in 1987. She attended UC Irvine, graduating as a Phi Beta Kappa (just like her dad, ha!). She married Kevin Grier in 1991. They have three children: Sarah (currently attending Carlton College, Scott (a junior at Dublin High School), and Rachel (currently in the eighth grade). Catheryn received an MA degree from

Cal State, and Kevin has his Ph.D. After living in Santa Maria and Rancho Cucamonga, they currently live in Dublin, California. Judy and I celebrated anniversary number 25 in 1990.

Mark graduated from St. Joseph in 1989. He attended UC San Diego and graduated in 1993. He later received an MA from the University of Southern California. He works in the movie business and is currently the vice president of International Publicity for Universal. He lives in Los Angeles.

Judy retired from Allan Hancock College in 2005, and we moved from Westrail Estates to the Rice Ranch development in 2014.

10.0-4. Celebration: Anniversary number 25!

10.0-5. Family photo at Mark's, Christmas 2016.

10.0-6. Three grandkids, Sarah, Scott, and Rachel, Thanksgiving 2017

CHAPTER 11

Retirement Years

I have been unsuccessful at retirement. I tried several times. It never seemed to agree with me. My first was when I retired from the United States Air Force. My official retirement was 30 April 1985 (twenty years of service—to the day). After I retired, I taught part-time for several colleges and universities. I taught business management, leadership, and organizational development for

11.0-1. Retirement, Major General Don Henderson presiding

Allan Hancock College, West Coast University, Chapman University (MA level), and University of San Francisco (graduate and undergraduate organizational development.)

Shortly after retiring, I did some consulting first with the City of Solvang (First Human Relations handbook), French Hospital, and the Marian Medical Center. In 1989 I worked Burke O'Connor Associates on an organizational workload assessment for the Santa Barbara County Fire Department. In 1992 and 1993 I was the principal at Cuyama Valley High School (CVHS). CVHS is a small comprehensive high school. It was a lot of fun working with the kids, crowning the homecoming queen, etc.

In 1993, I went back to consulting with The Walker Group (TWG). TWG was a nationwide organization specializing in organizational redesign for large firms that had a high volume of customer turnover. I worked in the Midwest/Chicago area on a project with Continental Cable. In 1994/95 I worked on a project with the San Francisco Chronicle for over eighteen months.

I did some minor proposal work for Lockheed in 1991 and 1996 when they were bidding on the Western Test Range contract. I found that proposal work was right on my sweet spot. In 1997 I began working full-time as a proposal manager for Lockheed Martin starting in 1997 in Sunnyvale, California. After the Sunnyvale Office closed, I got on the proposal travel team. Some of the assignments were in California (Oxnard and San Diego), some in New Jersey (Cherry Hill), a number in Maryland (Seabrook, Rockville), some in Texas (Houston) and some in Virginia (Chantilly). I retired from Lockheed Martin in 2012.

11.0-2. Principal, Cuyama Valley High School

After Lockheed Martin, I worked with ASRC Federal from 2014 through January 2019; ASRC is headquartered in Beltsville, Maryland. I was able to do much of the work from home. During this time, I tried volunteering at the Marian Medical Center. I decided that volunteer work was not my cup of tea.

It wasn't all work and no play. Starting 1995 Judy and I have had season tickets to the San Francisco 49ers home games.

During the last twenty years, we made several trips to Bermuda, as well as vacations to the beach in Newport Beach, San Diego, and Pismo. Thanksgivings have been spent in Pebble Beach and the Bay area.

11.0-3. On the field, meeting with Sourdough Sam

11.0-4. Bermuda, our favorite vacation spot

CHAPTER 12

My Favorites

Favorite radio show (as a child): *The Lone Ranger*
Favorite food: hamburger
Favorite seafood: shrimp, salmon
Favorite Mexican food: cheese enchiladas
Favorite Italian Food: pepperoni pizza, Judy's lasagna, Angel Hair Pasta
Favorite drink: Manhattan on the rocks
Favorite movies: *Casablanca, The Guns of Navarone*
Favorite Western movies: *High Noon, Shane, Tombstone*
Favorite actor: Charlton Heston
Favorite actress: Doris Day
Favorite political figures: Ronald Reagan, Barry Goldwater
Favorite historical figure: Douglas MacArthur
Favorite books: American Caesar, James A. Michener books
Favorite cars:

- 1989 Honda Prelude with all-wheel steering, medium blue
- 2015 Nissan Altima SL, white
- 1989 Toyota pickup truck, dark gray
- 2012 Toyota Camry, dust gold
- 1957 Studebaker Silver Hawk, white/purple

Favorite Major League baseball team: Baltimore Orioles
Favorite National Football League team: Baltimore Colts
Favorite college football team: Maryland Terrapins, Ohio State Buckeyes, Alabama Crimson Tide

Favorite biblical verses: Psalm 23, II Chronicles 7:14, 121 Psalm, Ecclesiastes 10:2

The *Lord* is my shepherd; I shall not want. He maketh me to lie down in green pastures; he leadeth me beside the still waters. He restoreth my soul; he leadeth me in the paths of righteousness for his name's sake. Yea, though I walk through the valley of the shadow of death, I will fear no evil; for thou art with me; thy rod and thy staff they comfort me. Thou preparest a table before me in the presence of mine enemies; thou anointest my head with oil; my cup runneth over. Surely goodness and mercy shall follow me all the days of my life; and I will dwell in the house of the *Lord* forever." (*23 Psalm*)

If my people, who are called by my name, will humble themselves and pray and seek my face and turn from their wicked ways, then I will hear from heaven, and I will forgive their sin and will heal their land. (*11 Chronicles 7:14*)

I will lift up mine eyes unto the hills, from whence cometh my help. My help cometh from the Lord, which made heaven and earth. (*121 Psalm*)

A wise man's heart inclines to the right, but the heart of a fool to the left. (*Ecclesiastes 10:2*)

CHAPTER 13

Words of Wisdom— Life Advice

I am not sure what is my life advice is to the world. Suffice to say, I never tried to take life too seriously. So I leave you with some notable quotes I have tried to live by (some heavy, some not):

> *It doesn't cost anything to have good manners.*

> *There is no right way to do a wrong thing.*

> *As Mason said to Dixon, "You need to draw a line somewhere."*

> *Nothing that results from human progress is achieved through unanimous consent. Those who are enlightened before the others are condemned to pursue that light despite the others. (Christopher Columbus)*

> *Until one is committed there is hesitancy, a chance to draw back, always ineffectiveness. Concerning all acts of initiative and creation there is one elementary truth—the ignorance of which kills countless ideas and splendid plans. That the moment one commits oneself then providence moves also. All sorts of things occur to help that otherwise never would have occurred. A whole stream of events occurs from the decision in ones'*

favor. Unforeseen incidents, meetings, and material assistance happen which no one would have dreamt comes their way. (W. H. Murray)

If you always do what you always did, you will always get what you always got.

"Whatever you can do or believe that you can, begin it. Boldness has genius, power and even magic in it." (Goethe)

Never bet on a racehorse named "Tripod."

Treat everyone with dignity and respect.

The five R's—reading, writing, arithmetic, responsibility, and respect.

Don't get caught watching the paint dry.

The customer is always right.

If you take life too seriously, you will drive yourself crazy.

"It's easy to get the players. Getting 'em to play together—that's the hard part." (Casey Stengel)

"When you reach a fork in the road, take it." (Yogi Berra)

In the land of the blind, the one-eyed man is king.

Attachments

Cooper Chronicles

A Family Record of

John George Kuper (Cooper) and Elizabeth Zimmerman his Wife.
Unto the Third and Fourth Generation.

1. John George Kupper (Cooper) came from Strasbourg in the Alsace-
    Lorraine distrct of what was then Germany. He probably came
    earlier from Switzerland. His Passports were dated 1741 at
    Strasbourg, but the shipping records at Philadelphia say he
    arrived at Philadelphia from Rotterdam in 1751.
    His wife's named was Elizabeth Zimmerman, daughter of Michael
    Zimmerman. They both lie buried on the hillside, near where
    they settled on the Cooper homestead after the French and Indian
    War about 1769. A marble monument marks their resting place,
    put there by his great-great-grandson in 1929 when he sold the
    farm , reserving the square rod burial ground and free access
    thereto. The farm was in the Cooper name for 160 years, and the
    burial ground always preserved.
        The place was originally settled by Peter Long who
    says he was driven out by the Indians in 1756, and he sold his
    rights and improvements to John George Kupper in 1769, for fifty
    shillings.
        John George Kupper (Cooper) and Elizabeth his wife
    had six children:
    (a.) John Adam Cooper, born July 1, 1759,
                            died Nov.11, 1823. Age 64 yrs.
        He and Ludwig Schott, Jr. joined the Continental Army
        during the Revolutionary War under Captain Martin Weaver.
        After their return from the war he married the sister of
        Ludwig Schott, Jr. , Katrina Schott, a daughter of Ludwig
        Schott, Sr., who had settled near the present Shiffer's
        Mill, long known as Schott's Mill.
        They were married at St. David's Reformed Church in 1783.
        by Rev. Samuel Dubendorf. They had six children.

    (b.) Anna Maria Cooper, a daughter who was married to George
        Motter. They had a son, David Motter, who lived near
        Motter's U. B. Church, east of Elizabethville.
        A grandson, Jacob Motter, lived on Main Street, Elizabeth-
        ville, near the Cross Roads.

    (c.) Catherine Cooper, a daughter was married to Andrew Brown.
        Have no further records.

    (d.) Elizabeth Cooper, a daughter, was married to Abram Young.
        Have no further records.

    (e.) Jacob Cooper, a son. The only information I now have is
        his release for the farm to John Adam Cooper.

    (f.) Magdalena Cooper, a daughter maiden lady. The only infor-
        mation I now have is her release for the farm to John
        Adam Cooper.

2. John Adam Cooper and Katrina Schott his wife.

John Adam Cooper, as stated on the first page, was the eldest son of John George Cooper and Elizabeth Zimmerman, his wife. He was about ten years old when his parents moved to the Cooper Homestead farm in 1769. It was not until 1806 that the present house was built. The old log hut at the foot of the hill below the barn is said to have had no floor in it. We still have daffodils that came out of their garden. Katrina was a daughter of Ludwig Schott, Sr. whose family was also driven out by the Indians in 1756. But they returned after peace was declared. As said before, they had six children.

(a.) Elizabeth Cooper, their first born was taken on horseback to St. David's Reformed Church to be baptized, by Rev. Samuel Dubendorf, who had married them in 1783. At the church a young man named John Shoop took the baby from her mother's arms so she could get off the horse. Then her mother said to him: "Now if you wait for her to grow up, you can have her for your wife". He said he would, and he did. They were married and settled near the Elizabethvill-Carsonville Road in Small Valley.

(b.) Christiana Cooper, their second daughter was married to Jacob Weaver. They left a well known family in the lower end of Lykens Valley.

(c.) George Cooper, the older son lived on the farm adjoining the Cooper Homestead farm, which was originally a part of the same tract which was bought from Peter Long for fifty shillings. The Adam Cooper of Armstrong Valley was his son, Mrs. Fitting, James Cooper, Tom Cooper, Harry Cooper, and Mrs. Glace of Matamoras were grandchildren of George Cooper.

(d.) Margaret Cooper, a daughter was married to John Shorra (Jury) of near Millersburg. Jonas Jury, who lived on their homestead was a son. John Jury, a grandson, and Katie, Daisy, and Annie Jury are her great-grandchildren.

(e.) Catharine Cooper, a daughter was married to Michael Matter. Daniel, Ellen, Mrs. Jacob Jury, of Killinger, and Mrs. Emma Jane Ahren, the children of Levi Matter, the blacksmith of Matterstown, were grandchildren of Michael Matter's.

(f.) John Cooper, the younger son was married to Mary Miller. They lived on the Homestead farm and had nine children.

74

8.   John Cooper and Mary Miller his wife.

John Cooper was the youngest son of John Adam Cooper and his
wife Katrina Schott. He was 65 years old when the writer
was born, and we were close companions until I was 14 years
of age. They had nine children.

(a.) Jacob Cooper, the oldest son was married to Lydia Longabach.
      They had five children,- Leah, Mary, Rebecca, Emma, and
      John Henry. & *Amanda*.

(b.) Philip Cooper, second son, was married to Elizabeth Matter.
      They had six children,- Aaron, Josephine, Christiana, John,
      Allen and Katherine.

(c.) Amos Cooper, third son, was married to Anna Mary Motter.
      They had eleven children,- Daniel, Isabelle, Sarah, Susan,
      Polly, Elmira, Uriah, Munroe, Julia, Fannie, and Amos.

(d.) Gemima Cooper, was married to Daniel Lebo.
           They had three children,- John, Amanda, and Jacob.
           Cooper.
(e.) Nellie, ~~Cxxxxxxx~~ was married to Eli Swab.
      They had seven children,- Philip, Allen, Hannah, Amanda,
      Isaiah, Mary, and George.

(f.) Mary, Married to Josiah Miller.
           They had five children,- Josephine, John P. Joel,
      Henry and Ida.

(g.) William Cooper, married to Mary Martin.
           They had eight children,- Gemima, Abraham, Elma, Mary,
      William, Harry Edward, and Edith.

(h.) Silas Cooper, Married to Elizabeth Martin.
           They had four children, - Samuel, Edwin, Charles,
           and Estella.

(i.) Amanda, married to Henry Hartman.
           They had no children.

(1) JOHN GEORGE COOPER
Emigrated from
Strasburg, Germany. *1741*
B._____
D._____

His children were:
a.-John Adam Cooper
  B._____
  D._____
  m.-Katrina Schettin
b.-Anna Maria
  B._____
  D._____
  m.-George Motter
c.-Catharine
  B._____
  D._____
  m.-Andrew Brown
d.-Elizabeth
  B._____
  D._____
  m.-Abraham Young
e.-Jacob Cooper
  B._____
  D._____
  m.-_____
f.-Magdalena
  B._____
  D._____
  m.-_____

(2) JOHN ADAM COOPER
B.-July 1, 1759
D.-Nov.11, 1823
m.-Katrina Schettin

Their children were:
a.-Elizabeth
  B._____
  D._____
  m.-John Shoop
b.-Christiana
  B.___*1807(?)*___
  D._____
  m.-Jacob Weaver
c.-George Cooper
  B._____
  D._____
  m.-_____
d.-Margaret
  B._____
  D._____
  m.-John Sherra
e.-Catharine
  B._____
  D._____
  m.-Michael Matter
f.-John Cooper
  B._____
  D._____
  m.-Mary Miller

(3) JOHN COOPER
B._____
D._____
m.-Mary Miller

Their children were:
a.-Jacob Cooper
  B._____
  D._____
  m.-Lydia Longabach
b.-Philip Cooper
  B._____
  D._____
  m.-Eliz. Matter
c.-Amos Cooper
  B._____
  D._____
  m.-Mary A.Motter
d.-Gemima
  B._____
  D._____
  m.-Daniel Lebo
e.-Nellie
  B._____
  D._____
  m.-Eli Swab
f.-Mary
  B._____
  D._____
  m.-Josiah Miller
g.-William Cooper
  B._____
  D._____
  m.-Mary Martin
h.-Silas Cooper
  B._____
  D._____
  m.-Eliz. Martin.
i.-Amanda
  B._____
  D._____
  m.-Henry Hartman

The STORY of LOVER'S ROCK.

The Story of Lover's Rock varies with the locality, as well as with
the story teller. The one who told me the story of Millersburg's
Lovers Rock was my friend Mr. N. C.Freck about fifty years ago.
Where he got it I know not, but I often accused him of telling "old
time stories" as if they were new, by simply changing then so as to
look new. He seldom told them twice the same way.

This particular rock is on top of Berry's Mountain, east
of ta gap and about opposite the electric light plant. Mr. Freck
had timbered off a large tract of the mountain in the same vicin-
ity but a few years before he told me the story. I never saw the
story in print until about twenty years ago Mr. Barrett gave a stor
somewhat similar in character in his Pictorial Review of Lykens
and illiams Valley. He laid the scenes opposite Lykens. It is
entirely possible that the two stories originated with the same
band of Indians.
Some time between 1754 and 1760 two young English
boys are said to have come across the gap in the mountain and down
over the old Indian Trail to where a small stream enters the Wicon-
isco Creek. They found a band of Indians encamped there temporari-
ly. From the Chief they learned he was heading eastward to an
Indian village near the end of the valley. After their interview
withe the Chief they conversed between themselves and were surprised to hear a young lady inside the tent singing in plain
English. She recited in song that she had been captured by the
Indians, and they were bound for an Indian Village farther up in th
the valley where they proposed to wed her to the Chief's son, and
begged them to help her escape. By conversation loud enough so
she could hear it they said they would return in a little while,

77

LOVER'S ROCK. (continued)

and let her know a plan to carry her away from the Indians.
They returned about an hour later, and just outside of the Chief's
tent they spoke each to the other in English that they would have
two of the Indian's ponies as close to the Camp as seemed safe, and
if she could come that far they would stake their own lives on
freeing her. She replied in song that she would be "on the spot"
at the risk of her life.

After the boys were gone she kneeled in prayer to God
for protection, and when the Chief appeared on the scene she begged
for permission to go a little distance from the tent into the bushes by herself to pray to her own Great Spirit. Permission was
granted and the boys were ready with two Indian ponies which they
had stolen from the Indians. When she knelt down in the bushes
one of the boys picked her up and put her on a pony, and mounting
back of her, they went up the hollow and mountain-side over the old
Indian Trail as fast as the pony could travel.

The other boy rolled up their blanket in form like a
woman, and putting it in fron of himself, he mounted the other pony
and rode toward the River. The ruse worked all right, but he had
to ride through an open space, and when the braves discovered him
they followed in hot pursuit. Somewhere around the end of the
mountain they caught up with him and one of their arrows left a
mortal wound. They discovered they had tracked the wrong boy,
and they turned back, chasing the other one up the mountain trail.

In the meantime the boy with the young lady companion
had reached the top of the mountain, but had lost the trail and
proceeded eastward to the top of the peak above the gap. Going
down eastward, just before they reached the large rock, known as

LOVERS ROCK (continued.)

Lovers Rock, the pony fell and broke his leg. In the excitement
what to do next they sought for a hiding place beneath that big
rock. But just then they heard his brother calling at the foot
of the mountain toward Fort Halifax. They hastened down the
mountain, and there found his brother with the other pony. He
wanted his brother to take the young lady and he would follow on fo
foot. But he said, nay, I am mortally wounded and will have but
a few hours more to live. You and the lady will get on the pony
and flee for Fort Halifax. I will go up the mountain and head off
the Indians until you are safe beyond there reach.

It appears the brothers looked so nearly alike that even
an Indian could not tell them apart, having seen them only once.
When the older brother started up the mountain the other and the
young lady mounted the pony and fled toward Fort Halifax.
The older brother did not reach the top of the mountain before
the band of Indian braves met him. They insisted that he tell
them where the girl is. He told them she was fatally injured in
fall from the pony when he broke his leg, and that he had hid her
behind the big rock. They made him go along and show them where,
and when they failed to find her he said she must have revived
and was probably hiding in the bushes near by. It was near evening
now, and as the sun was setting he climbed on top of Lovers Rock
to see the sun go down for the last time. After the sun went down
he fell down a lifeless body. The Indians search until dark, but
only found they had been hoaxed again, when they discovered the
arrow wound on his body.

The next day a party from the Fort started in search of

LOVERS ROCK. (Continued)

stretched out and covered with a few branches from surrounding
bushes.   "Rock of Ages cleft for me",
         "Let me hide myself in Thee". -- When the Sun goes down.

While they were getting ready to remove the body they were
startled with a sound in the bushes, and a lone Indian appeared,
the young Prince who was to marry their captive lady.

It appears that the love of an Indian can be as stead-
fast as that of any paleface.   That morning the Indians broke
camp and started eastward up the Valley toward the old Indian
Village above what is now Loyalton, but the young Prince refused
to go until he had further satisfied himself that his lady love
was gone. When the rescuers assured him that she had gone beyond
his reach he followed his band in a half dazed condition, and the
party from the Fort removed the body of the brave English boy and
buried it.
Here Mr. Freck's story ended. I never saw it in history. It is probably not recorded, as during those years the air
was full of Indian stories, and Mr. Freck was known to tell Idian
stories to his Sunday School Class when interest seemed to lag
with his boys. The story seems to good to be forgotten. That is
my apology for writing it.

History records that about the same time an Indian maraud-
ing party went up through the valley, drove out Ludwig Schutt near
what is now Shiffer's Mill, Peter Lang from the farm known as the
Cooper homestead, and fought a battle with Andrew Lycans, Schutt
and others near Loyalton.   What became of our Indian Prince no one
knows, except that several years later a lone Indian appeared on
opposite bank of the Creek near my great-great-grandmothers home,
(the Cooper homstead) and called to her, aiming a gun, but said

LOVERS ROCK,(Continued)

he only wanted to scare her. He was apparently demented and
harmless. He was seen a nuber of places under strange conditions
for several years, and may have been the same Indian Prince.
The girl's story unlike that of Regina Hartmann seems entirely
lost, but then she got married to her boy rescuer, and maybe that
explains why she was not heard of any more. I never heard her
maiden name.

                    S. W. Coper,
                              Baltimore, Md.
          Sept. 7, 1942.

Newspaper Clipping

------------------ Telegram.

Millersburg, Feb. 6. A strange and mysterious happening occurred in this town on Thursday, which while few indeed will credit, is vouched for by men of truth. On Thursday morning there was a jovial crowd in a certain hotel at this place, and while they were imbibing, as your correspondent was told, Samuel Motter entered. Motter is well known throughout this county as a patent medicine peddler, and is about 55 years aid of age. His wife died in the almshouse sometime ago, and since then he has been living near this place. Shortly after Motter entered the bar-room a discussion on religious subjects ensued and the sacrament of the Lord's Supper was talked about. Motter became very earnest in his talk and finally dared the men to indulge in an improvised supper.
The men agreed to have it with beer and bread, and accordingly a glass of that beverage was filled. Then they kneeled in mock humility, and with the beer in one hand and the bread in the other, Motter went a along distributing a bite and a sip to each.
Suddenly, when he got about through, a strange noise was heard, and looking up the men saw a sight that made their blood run cold and froze the marrow of their bones. As near as the scared men can descri describe it they declare it was an immense illy-formed and foul beast with great cloven feet, pointed horns and eyes that flashed fire. with wild yells the men rushed out into the open air and scattered in every direction . Finally all of them got tp their homes but Motter, who was away for a long time. At last he arrived a maniac. He was put to bed and a physician summoned, but they could do nothing for that stricken brain. He raved and howled and prayed in the most maniacal manner, declaring that he had seen the evil one and that he was lost. His torture was terrific and awful, but nothing could be done to relieve him, and after enduring this horrible mental pain and misery he died in the wildest agony imaginable. That death-bed scene is said to have been full of horrors that can hardly be conceived.
This is the version of the account as given to your correspondent.

By S. . . C. :- I remember well the excitement that was raised at the time, I would say it was about 1880. Motter was a well known ch charac ter. I had never seen it in the newspaper at the time, but recently copied the aboute from a newspaper clipping that had been preserved. A letter even came from Canada at the time inquiring about the truth of the occurrence. I knew most of the men who were said to have been connected with it, as well as the hotel and its landlord. Ofcourse, they all denied having been in it.

1918 —Elizabeth Cooper (Papa Cooley's mother) with Betty Sehrt

Sehrt Chronicles

HENRY SEHRT AND FAMILY

Henry Sehrt , born 28 Feb 1856 in Wolzhausen, Hesse, Germany, was the second son of Balthazar and Anna Elisabeth Sehrt. According to Lula Cameron, Henry's father and grandfather were school principals. As a young man, Henry was conscripted into the German army where he served as a paymaster. This unwelcome civil obligation was one of his reasons for emigrating from Germany to the United States. Henry came. alone, sailing from Bremen on .the S.S. Kronprinz Frederick Wilhelm and arrived at the port of Baltimore on 28 May 1881. The passenger list to be seen on microfilm at the National Archives (Microfilm 255, Roll 33, p. 17 #734) has the following information:
Name: Heinr. Sehrt
Age:25
Occupation - merchant
Country to which they belong - Hessia
Destination: Baltimore

According to Lula,Henry had a job upon arrival in Baltimore at the grocery store on Eastern Avenue of an uncle who spelled his name Sert. Uncle Charles Sehrt, however, had a different story. He gave his nephew, Norman Cameron, a photograph,now in my possession,of Henry Sehrt in front of a grocery store with the accompanying message: "Grandfather Henry Sehrt's first job in the U.S. (circa 1882-1884) was at this grocery store at corner of Asquith and Lexington Sts., Baltimore, MD. Henry Sehrt is standing 2nd from left in white shirt sleeves and vest." The name on the pictured store is J.H.Heyn & Co and below that "Horn & Brother - fine family groceries - canned goods" The horse drawn delivery carriage standing beside the building says "JNO. H. HEYN & CO - GROCERS" The store is on the first floor of a 3-story brick building with an iron railed balcony on the second floor front.

The 1882 Directory for Baltimore shows the following:
Henry SERT, grocery, Eastern Avenue near Third
Henry SEHRT, clerk, 218 Aliceanna
The 1885 directory also lists Henry SERT, grocer, on Eastern Avenue
By 1890 the directory say Henry SEHRT, grocer, 237 Eastern Avenue
so perhaps Lula's story that Henry Sehrt bought a grocery store from an uncle who spelled his name differntly is the correct one. Maybe Henry clerked at Heyn & Co before working for Sert. Anyhow he became the pro- prietor of a grocery store and at some point opened a hardware store at the same location.
The 1899 Directory Has Henry Sehrt, grocer, at a slightly different address on Eastern, #225 instead of 237. There is also a Caroline Sehrt listed as "dressmaker, 1301 E. Lafayette Avenue". Is this Henry's wife?

In 1884 Henry married Caroline Becker, daughter of Henry and Louisa, They had three sons - Ed, Charlie, and another who died in infancy - and two daughters - Lula and Eva. The latter, born in 1899, did not reach her 5th birthday. Lula believed that she died of Bright's disease.

The 1900 Census (Vol.7, E.D. 54, Sheet 21, line 81) shows the following:
Henry Sehrt, age 44, head of household
227 Eastern Avenue, Baltimore   Born Feb. 1856 Germany (naturalized)
Caroline Sehrt, b May 1858, age 42, b. Md.
Edward Sehrt, son, age 12, born March 1888 Md.
Charles   "   "   "   9,   "   July 1890 Md.
Lulu Sehrt, daughter, age 6, born Aug 1893 Md.
Eva Sehrt   "   " 10/12   born Aug 1899 Md.

State of Maryland,

Circuit Court for Baltimore County, to wit:

BE IT REMEMBERED, That on the _thirtieth_ day of _May_ in the year eighteen hundred and _eighty eight_ _Henry Sehrt_ a native of _Hesse Darmstadt_ personally appeared in the Clerk's Office of said Circuit Court, and makes oath on the Holy Evangely of Almighty God, that it is bona fide his inten-t} to become a

CITIZEN OF THE UNITED STATES,

and to renounce and abjure forever all allegiance and fidelity to every foreign Prince, Potentate, State and Sovereignty whatever, and particularly all allegiance and fidelity to the _Emperor of Germany_ of whom he was heretofore a subject.

IN TESTIMONY WHEREOF I have hereto set my hand and affixed the seal of my office, this _30th_ day of _May_ in the year of our Lord one thousand eight hundred and _eighty eight_

John W Shanklin
Clerk of the Circuit Court for Baltimore County.

Wm. H. Ruby, Print.

The census report also stated that Henry and Caroline had been married 16 yrs., that he emigrated in 1881, that his occupation was grocer, that he owned his home, and that he could read, write and speak English. In the household there was a servant named Annie Reing, born August 1885 in Germany, emigrated to the U.S in 1900. Fresh off the boat, so to speak. Lula remembered this girl as having a round face with red cheeks and said that Ed & Charlie teased her a great deal.

Lula said that for many years the Sehrts lived at 3425 Eastern Avenue. This was their address as late as 1914. Did the numbering system for houses change or did the family move farther out Eastern Avenue after 1900? By 1920 Henry & Caroline lived at 2925 Overland Avenue at the corner of Harford Road.

Photos of Henry in later years show a short, slim, sober gentleman with a small moustache and neat, short hair. In my opinion, Uncle Ed looked very like his father, but Ed was considerably taller. All Henry's children, even Lula, grew to be taller than he. In none of the photos is Henry smiling, but perhaps he was as jolly as his two sons were.

Lula described her father as a scholarly man who often said that, if he had his life to live over, he would have been a history teacher instead of a merchant. Henry Sehrt played the piano and all of his children were musical: Ed played the piano and violin; Charlie played the cornet, trombone, cello and piano; Lula played the piano. *

Henry did not get back to Germany while his mother was alive; a failure he always regretted. She died in 1904, so it must have taken him more than 25 years to re-cross the Atlantic. The date of his first return trip is not known to me, but in 1910 he returned taking Caroline and Lula. Lula remembered meeting her uncles, aunts and their families, and she became fiends with some of her cousins. I believe she especially liked Rudolph and Matilde Fischer, children of Aunt Maggie Sehrt Fischer. She met Johanna Sehrt and Matilde Velte, Uncle Karl's daughters, but they were 11 or 12 years her senior. The Fischers lived in Marburg and Uncle Karl's family in Lollar béi Giessen. Uncle Rudolph Sehrt was the postmaster in Offenbach. Lula accompanied her father to Germany in 1914, the year Ed was studying at Leipsig, and I enclose clippings to illustrate how poor that timing was!

Lula said her father signed his name "Hy. Sehrt".
His wife pre-deceased him by six years. Sometime after her death, he moved in with Charles and Mabel, for his residence at the time of his death in 1935 is given as 2401 Mayfield Avenue. From the death certificate it appears that Henry died from the effects of diabetes and chronic myocarditis. He left his three children a sizeable estate, especially by those Depression year standards. I do not know when Henry retired, but Charles took over the grocery and hardware business for him.

* In the style of those pre-radio and television days, the children often played ensemble while friends and family gathered around the living room to sing or listen.

This Sehrt line of descent comes from a book written on the Sehrt family
by a German descendant who contacted Uncle Ed Sehrt. He, in turn, photo-
copied some pages for us, but it is all in German. Unfortunately, Ed did
not say and I neglected to ask the name of the book or the author. Very
poor research by me!

Hans Sehrt b. 1600
   ↓
Curt Sehrt m. CAtharina Schmidt
   ↓
Johannes Sehrt m.1714 Catharina Keil
   ↓
Konrad Sehrt m. 1740 Anna Schnabel in Atzenhain, Germany
   ↓
Wilhelm Sehrt m. Elisabeth Stoffel
   ↓
Wiegand Sehrt m. Christine Seng in Atzenhain
   1791-1854?
   ↓
Balthazar Sehrt m. Anna Elisabeth Schneider (Lehrerstochter - teacher's daughter)
   1827-1873   1828-1904
   ↓
Heinrich (Henry) Sehrt m. 1884 Caroline Becker
   1856-1935   1858-1929
   ↓
Charles George Sehrt m. 1916 Mabel E. Cooper
   1890-1986   1890-1959
   ↓
Elizabeth A. Sehrt m. 1940 Simeon Markline
   1917-   1916-1944
   ↓
Charles Markline
   1942-

FAMILY GROUP NO. _____

Husband's Full Name Henry Sehrt

This Information Obtained From:	Husband's Data	Day Month Year	City, Town or Place	County or Province, etc.	State or Country	Add. Info. on Husband
Lula Sehrt Cameron	Birth	28 Feb 1856	Wolzhausen	Hesse	Germany	Immigrated
Edwart H. Sehrt	Chr'nd					to USA in
Betty S. Sperry	Marr.	1884				1881
1900 Census	Death	5 Nov 1935	Baltimore		MD	
Baltimore and Loudon	Burial	Loudon Park Cemetery, Baltimore, MD				
Park Cemeteries	Places of Residence	Germany, Baltimore				
National Archives	Occupation Merchant			Church Affiliation Lutheran?..	Military Rec. Paymaster in
ship passenger list				Presbyterian	German Army
HH:128-18-733	His Father Balthasar Sehrt			Mother's Maiden Name Elizabeth Schneider
75th Anniversary booklet						
of Abbott Memorial	**Wife's Full Maiden Name** Caroline Baker					
Presbyterian Church	Wife's Data	Day Month Year	City, Town or Place	County or Province, etc.	State or Country	Add. Info. on Wife
	Birth	5 May 1858	Baltimore		MD	
	Chr'nd					
	Death	9 May 1929	Baltimore		MD	
	Burial	Loudon Park Cemetery, Baltimore, MD				
Compiler Roedah Cameron	Places of Residence Baltimore					
Address	Occupation		Church Affiliation		Military Rec.	
City, State	Other husbands, if any. No. (1) (2) etc. Make separate sheet for each marr.					
Date March 1999	Her Father Henry Baecker			Mother's Maiden Name Louisa.		

Sex	Children's Names in Full (Arrange in order of birth)	Children's Data	Day Month Year	City, Town or Place	County or Province, etc.	State or Country	Add. info. on Children
	1 Son.	Birth					
		Marr.					
	Full Name of Spouse	Death	died in infancy				
		Burial					
	2 Edward Henry	Birth	3 Mar 1888	Baltimore		MD	Had one
		Marr.	① 1915 ② Sept 1961				daughter,
	Full Name of Spouse ① Cecelia Shane. ② Helen Ludwig	Death	20 Nov 1986	McLean		VA	Cecelia
		Burial	Loudon Park Cemetery, Baltimore			MD	1916-1928
	3 Charles George	Birth	2 July 1890	Baltimore		MD	Had two
		Marr.	① 24 Oct 1916 ② 1961				daughters -
	Full Name of Spouse ① Mabel Cooper ② Kay Kraft	Death	Nov 1964	Baltimore.		MD	Betty +
		Burial	Loudon Park Cemetery, Baltimore.			MD	Mary Louise
	4 Louise Marguerite	Birth	29 Aug 1893	Baltimore		MD	Had son,
		Marr.	11 Aug 1920	Baltimore		MD	Norman and
	Full Name of Spouse Norman W. Cameron	Death	28 Nov 1989	Gaithersburg Montgomery Co.		MD.	daughter,
		Burial	Loudon Park Cemetery, Baltimore			MD	Caroline.
	5 Eva	Birth	Aug 1899	Baltimore		MD	
		Marr.					
	Full Name of Spouse	Death	circa 1904	Baltimore		MD	
		Burial					
	6	Birth					
		Marr.					
	Full Name of Spouse	Death					
		Burial					
	7	Birth					
		Marr.					
	Full Name of Spouse	Death					
		Burial					
	8	Birth					
		Marr.					
	Full Name of Spouse	Death					
		Burial					
	9	Birth					
		Marr.					
	Full Name of Spouse	Death					
		Burial					
	10	Birth					
		Marr.					
	Full Name of Spouse	Death					
		Burial					

* For additional children use Everton Publishers' Children Continuation Sheet, Form A11

FAMILY GROUP No. _____ Husband's Full Name _Henry Sehrt_

This Information Obtained From:

	Husband's Data	Day Month Year	City, Town or Place	County or Province, etc.	State or Country	Add. Info. on Husband
Louise S. Cameron	Birth	28 Feb 1856	Wolzhausen	Hesse	Germany	
Edward H. Sehrt	Chr'nd					
Loudon Park Cemetery	Mar.	1884				
1900 Census	Death	5 Nov 1935	Baltimore		MD	
Betty Sperry	Burial	Loudon Park Cemetery, Baltimore			MD	

Places of Residence Germany, Baltimore
Occupation Merchant   Church Affiliation Lutheran   Military Rec. Paymaster in German Army
Other wives, if any. No. (1) (2) etc. Make separate sheet for each mar.
His Father Balthazar Sehrt   Mother's Maiden Name Anna Elis. Schneider

Wife's Full Maiden Name _Caroline Baker_

	Wife's Data	Day Month Year	City, Town or Place	County or Province, etc.	State or Country	Add. Info. on Wife
	Birth	5 May 1858	Baltimore		MD.	
	Chr'nd					
	Death	9 May 1929	Baltimore		MD	
	Burial	Loudon Park Cemetery, Baltimore			MD	

Places of Residence
Compiler Rolda Cameron
Address 15 Brook Court
City, State Summit, N.J.
Date 8-21-91

Occupation if other than Housewife   Church Affiliation
Other husbands, if any. No. (1) (2) etc. Make separate sheet for each mar.
Her Father Henry Baecker   Mother's Maiden Name Louisa

Sex	Children's Names in Full (Arrange in order of birth)	Children's Data	Day Month Year	City, Town or Place	County or Province, etc.	State or Country	Add. Info. on Children
	1 Edward Henry Full Name of Spouse* 1. Cecilia Schane 2. Helen Ludwig	Birth	3 Mar 1888	Baltimore		MD	One daughter, Cecilia, who died in childhood
		Mar.					
		Death	20 Nov 1986	Arlington		VA	
		Burial	Loudon Park Cemetery, Baltimore, MD				
	2 Charles George Full Name of Spouse* ① Mabel E. Cooper ② Kay Kraft	Birth	2 July 1890	Baltimore		MD	Two daughter by 1st wife, Betty and Mary Louise. Son Norman and daughter Caroline.
		Mar.	① 24 Oct 1916				
		Death	Nov 1986	Baltimore		MD	
		Burial	Loudon Park Cemetery, Baltimore, MD				
	3 Louise Marguerite Full Name of Spouse* Norman W. Cameron	Birth	27 Aug 1893	Baltimore		MD	
		Mar.	11 Aug 1920	"		"	
		Death	28 Nov 1989	Gaithersburg Montgomery Co.		MD	
		Burial	Loudon Park Cemetery, Baltimore			MD	
	4 Eva Full Name of Spouse*	Birth	Aug 1899	Baltimore		MD	
		Mar.					
		Death	1904				
		Burial					
	5 Full Name of Spouse*	Birth					
		Mar.					
		Death					
		Burial					
	6 Full Name of Spouse*	Birth					
		Mar.					
		Death					
		Burial					
	7 Full Name of Spouse*	Birth					
		Mar.					
		Death					
		Burial					
	8 Full Name of Spouse*	Birth					
		Mar.					
		Death					
		Burial					
	9 Full Name of Spouse*	Birth					
		Mar.					
		Death					
		Burial					
	10 Full Name of Spouse*	Birth					
		Mar.					
		Death					
		Burial					

*If married more than once No. each mar. (1) (2) etc. and list in "Add. Info. on children" column. Use reverse side for additional children, other notes, references or information.

FAMILY GROUP No. ____

Husband's Full Name *Henry Baecker*

This Information Obtained From:	Husband's Data	Day Month Year	City, Town or Place	County or Province, etc.	State or Country	Add. Info. on Husband
Baltimore Cemetery	Birth	7 Nov 1822			Germany	
Lala S. Cameron	Chr'nd					
Edward Sehrt	Mar.					
Death Certificates of	Death	27 Aug 1890	Baltimore,		MD	
Henry + Louisa.	Burial	Baltimore Cemetery, North Ave, Baltimore			MD	
1900 Census	Places of Residence Germany / Baltimore					
Margaret Baker	Occupation *Cabinetmaker* Church Affiliation				Military Rec.	
	Other wives, if any. No. (1) (2) etc. Make separate sheet for each mar.					
	His Father			Mother's Maiden Name		

Wife's Full Maiden Name *Louisa*

	Wife's Data	Day Month Year	City, Town or Place	County or Province, etc.	State or Country	Add. Info. on Wife
	Birth	22 Aug 1822 (G 1821?)			Germany	
	Chr'nd					
	Death	17 May 1909				
	Burial	Baltimore Cemetery North Ave., Baltimore, MD				
Compiler *Roedah Cameron*	Places of Residence Germany, Baltimore					
Address *15 Brook Court*	Occupation if other than Housewife			Church Affiliation		
City, State *Summit, NJ*	Other husbands, if any, No. (1) (2) etc. Make separate sheet for each mar.					
Date *8-21-91*	Her Father			Mother's Maiden Name		

Sex	Children's Names in Full (Arrange in order of birth)	Children's Data	Day Month Year	City, Town or Place	County or Province, etc.	State or Country	Add. Info. on Children
1	George	Birth	7 June 1850	Baltimore		MD	Daughters
	Full Name of Spouse*	Mar.					Caroline
	Gertrude	Death	8 Mar 1908	Baltimore		MD	and Emma
		Burial	Baltimore Cemetery				
2	Herman	Birth	15 Oct 1854				
	Full Name of Spouse*	Mar.	—				
		Death	9 Apr 1910				
		Burial	Baltimore Cemetery				
3	Caroline	Birth	5 May 1858	Baltimore		MD	4 children,
	Full Name of Spouse*	Mar.	1884	"		"	See chart
	Henry Sehrt	Death	9 May 1929	"		"	
		Burial	Loudon Park Cemetery, Baltimore			MD	
4	Henry J.	Birth	17 Aug 1863	Baltimore		MD	Son, Harry
	Full Name of Spouse*	Mar.					and daughter
	Eva Walling	Death	8 Mar 1904	Baltimore		MD	Bessie
		Burial					
5		Birth					
	Full Name of Spouse*	Mar.					
		Death					
		Burial					
6		Birth					
	Full Name of Spouse*	Mar.					
		Death					
		Burial					
7		Birth					
	Full Name of Spouse*	Mar.					
		Death					
		Burial					
8		Birth					
	Full Name of Spouse*	Mar.					
		Death					
		Burial					
9		Birth					
	Full Name of Spouse*	Mar.					
		Death					
		Burial					
10		Birth					
	Full Name of Spouse*	Mar.					
		Death					
		Burial					

*If married more than once No. each mar. (1) (2) etc. and list in "Add. info. on children" column. Use reverse side for additional children, other notes, references or information.

Prepared by R.M.Cameron with additions by Herta Velte

b = born
d = died
+ = married

SEHRT
1. Georg Karl
   b. 5 Oct 1863
   d. 6. Aug. 1940
   +
   Katharina Seim
   b. 13.11.1854
   d. 21.9.1925

2. Heinrich (Henry)
   b. 28 Feb 1856
   d. 5 Nov 1935
   +
   Caroline Baker
   b. 5 May 1858
   d. 9 May 1929

Balthasar Sehrt
b. 12 Mar 1827
d. 6.12.1873
+
Anna
Elizabeth Schneider
b. 6.11.1828 Schneider
d. 26.2.1904

3. Margarete
   b. 22 Feb 1858
   d.
   +
   John. Wm. Fischer
   b. 4 Apr 1854
   d. 12 Mar 1960

4. Rudolph
   b. 5 Oct 1862
   d. 30 Oct 1936
   +
   Elisabeth Schauss
   b.
   d.   1927

SEHRT
1. Albert - died as a child
2. Mathilde
   b. 24 Apr 1881
   d. 7 Feb 1951
   +
   Wilhelm Velte
   b. 27.81.1580
   d. 30.11.1976
3. Johanna
   b. 31 Oct. 1882
   d. 28. Okt. 1958

SEHRT
1. Edward H
   b. 5 Mar 1888, d. Nov. 1936
   +
   ① Cecilia Schane
   ② Helen Ludwig
2. Charles G.
   b. 2 July 1890   d. Nov 1976
   +
   ① Mabel Cooper
   ② Kay Kraft
3. Son - died in infancy
4. Louise M. "Lulu"
   b. 27 Aug 1893, d. Nov 1989
   + 1920
   Norman W. Cameron
   b. 27 Sept 1874
   d. 21 Nov 1947
5. Eva
   b. Aug 1899
   d.   1904

FISCHER
1. Rudolph
   b.

2. Mathilde
   b. 5 Nov. 1898
   d.
   +
   Carl Herdan
   b.
   d. 29. Nov. 1976

SEHRT
1. Karl
   b.
   d.

2. Hedwig
   b. 16 Mar 1899
   d.

VELTE
2. Herta
   b. 23.3.1911
   d.
1. Walther
   b. 27.12.1907
   d. 5.6. 1934
3. Wilhelm
   b. 4.12.1915
   d. 15.6. 1934

SEHRT
1. Cecelia
   b.   1917
   d. July 1928

SEHRT
1. Betty
   b. 19 Aug 1917
   +
   Charles Sperry
   b. 28 Apr. 1913
2. Mary Louise
   b. 7 Apr 1922
   +
   William Parks
   b. 2 Dec 1921
     + 1950

CAMERON
1. Norman W. Jr
   b. 28 Oct 1921
   d. 14 Nov 1992
   + 1950
   Roleah Northup
   b. 10 Apr 1929
2. Caroline M.
   b. 11 Dec 1922
   +
   b. 14 Mar 1926

HERDAN
1. Rudolph
   b.   1924
   d. W.W. II
2. Helmut
   b.
3. Margaret
   b.
   +

SEHRT
1. Richard   b. 5 Dec 1923
   killed in W.W. II
2. Norbert   b. 20 June 1920

94

"Pop" (Charles George Sehrt)—This "German" Christening
Certificate—German name "George Carl"

CERTIFICATE OF DEATH

MARYLAND

Name in Full: *Louisa Becker*

Died at *Highlandtown* County *Balto*

Date of death 190 *9* Month *5* Day *17* Age *57* Years Months Days

Sex *Female* Color or Race *White* Birthplace *Germany*

Occupation *None* Where Residing if not at place of death *3425 Eastern A*

Married, Single or Widowed *Widow* Name of Wife or Husband *Henry Becker*

Father's Name *Unknown* Father's Birthplace *Germany*

Mother's Maiden Name *Unknown* Mother's Birthplace *Germany*

Name of person giving Information *Mrs Henry Sehrt* How related to deceased *Daughter*

CAUSES OF DEATH

Primary *Apoplexy* How long *5 Days*

Immediate *Debility* How long *5 Days*

Are the name, age, sex, color, date and place correctly given above? *Yes*

Signature of Physician *Dr. F. A. Glantz* Address *3245 East Av.*

Filed 1909

Accident or Suicide

ghlandtown Spoke German

A. Niemitz

German was more widely spoken there than English, and when you walked down the street and heard everyone speaking it in front of stores that displayed imported German delicacies, you might have thought you were in Munich. One of the stores in which German was spoken was Henry Sehrt's, which also is pictured.

Uncle Ed, Henry Sehrt and Pop by the front door of the grocery store.
Article published in the Baltimore Sun.

96

CHARLES GEORGE SEHRT.

A Λ Φ

Member Orchestra, 07-'09; Secretary Orchestra, '08-09; Member Shakespearean Society; Member Chess Club.

Isn't he the grandest thing you ever saw? His hair is his fortune. You can't imagine how "cut up" he is when he is compelled to have his golden locks taken off. "Cutie" is somewhat of a mathematician, and can be seen taking long walks in the country with Steve Norris, who thinks that Sehrt is a prodigy. He also plays in the orchestra, and his one ambition is to become a member of the Park Band after he graduates from the City College. However, we wish Sehrt the greatest success in his musical pursuits, and sincerely hope that he will some day become the Mayor of Highlandtown.

"Pop"

NORTH GERMAN LLOYD
BALTIMORE SERVICE

TWIN-SCREW STEAMSHIP
FRIEDRICH DER GROSSE

LIST OF PASSENGERS
II CABIN
——— FROM ———
BALTIMORE TO BREMEN
JUNE 23rd, 1914

A. SCHUMACHER & COMPANY
GENERAL AGENTS
HANSA HAUS   BALTIMORE

Note the date—approximately 8 weeks before start of World War I.

Miss Alice Ropes
Miss Charlotte Ropes
Dr. John C. Rudolph
Mrs. Rudolph
Miss Etta Ruser
Mr. Emil Sass
Mrs. Sass
Mrs. Minnie F. Sauber
Mr. R. B. Scandrett, Jr.
Mrs. Scandrett
Miss Rebekah Scandrett
Miss Pauline Schaefer
Mrs. Carolina Schmelzle
Rev. Richard Schmidt
Mrs. Schmidt
        and infant
Miss Gertrude Schmidt
Mrs. Emilie Schmidt
Miss Anna Schmidt
Miss Lilly Schmidt
Mrs. Marie Schrader
Mr. Rudolph Schroeder
Mrs. Schroeder
Mr. Rudolph Schwab
Mrs. Rebecca Schwaber

Mr. Henry Sehrt
Miss Lula Sehrt
Mr. F. W. Seibold
Mrs. Seibold
Miss Bertha Sendelbach
Mrs. Emma Severin
Miss Clara Severin
Miss Sophie Seyboth
Miss Cecilia M. Shane
Mr. John Sperry
Mr. Edwin R. Stearns
Mrs. Stearns
Miss Anna R. Streckfuss
Mrs. Emma H. Stein
Miss Amy E. Stein
Miss Elizabeth R. Stoner
Miss Clara Stoyer
Dr. F. O. Sturhahn
Mrs. Sturhahn
Master Roland Sturhahn
Mr. Henry Newton Sweeting
Mrs. Lee Thurman

NO WORD FROM HER FAMILY IN EUROPE

Mrs. Sehrt Ill From Worry Over Absence of Husband, Son and Daughter.

THINKS ARE VISITING IN LEIPSIG, GERMANY

Government Reports Son Unknown in Leipsig; Is a Student There.

Made ill by worry over the absence in Europe of her husband, son and daughter, Mrs. Henry Sehrt is confined to her bed at her home, 3425 Eastern avenue. She believes they are in the interior of Germany, possibly at Leipsiz, but has heard nothing from them for five weeks past.

Appeal was made to the American government, through Congressman Talbott, more than a week ago, and this morning Mrs. Sehrt received a telegram from the State Department, Washington, D. C., stating that inquiries made by federal officials at Leipsig, especially concerning her son, Edward H. Sehrt, revealed that he is unknown there.

This information is regarded as absurd by Mrs. Sehrt and has greatly increased her fears. She says her son has been a student at the University of Leipsig for more than a year and that when he first went to Leipsig he had to report to the American consul.

Mrs. Sehrt's husband and daughter (Henry Sehrt and Miss Lula Sehrt) and a friend of the family (Miss Margaret Schane, a teacher at the Highlandtown Public School) went abroad two months ago, and have been traveling extensively in Italy, France and Germany. The last letter received by Mrs. Sehrt from them, about five weeks ago, told of their having reached Paris and of their plans to leave there in a few days for Leipsig to visit Edward Sehrt. The date on the letter indicated that the tourists had reached Paris about a week before war was declared between France and Germany, but it is believed sure, in view of the fact that no further word has been received from them, that they succeeded in reaching Leipsig.

Another appeal will be made to Congressman Talbott for further efforts by this government to locate them. Edward H. Sehrt's address, as given by Mrs. Sehrt, is "Drugerstrasse 55, Leipsig, Germany." There is a possibility, as Mrs. Sehrt admits, that he has been drafted for service in the Germany army.

TO INSPECT WARSHIP

SEHRTS SAFE IN BERLIN, GERMANY

Mrs. Sehrt Receives News From Her Husband, Son and Daughter.

News from Berlin, Germany, informing her of the safety of her husband, son and daughter in that city was received by Mrs. Henry Sehrt, 3425 Eastern avenue, Highlandtown, this morning, and has given her great relief. Mrs. Sehrt, as told in The Star yesterday, had been made ill by worry over the whereabouts of her relatives, having received no news from them for five weeks. The information received today was in the form of a letter from her daughter, Miss Lula Sehrt, who wrote as follows:

"Berlin, Germany, August 13, 1914.

"Dearest Mother and Charles:

"We are now in Berlin and perfectly safe. We could not write before because mails would not be forwarded unless written in German and left open. We do not know when we will get home, but hope to be able to get away about August 29 or September 5. Ships have been sent over, but everybody is making a grand rush for them. We just left the Ambassador's office to write this note and will give it to him to mail. So don't worry if you don't get mail. We will write as often as possible and will get home as soon as we can.

"Mr. and Mrs. Baehr, of Catonsville, are still with us, so we have a nice little party. Don't worry about us, for we are as safe as if in America, and we will have many experiences to tell you when we get home. Must close now so that this letter will be sent on the afternoon train. Love to both of you.

"(Signed) "LULA."

Miss Lula Sehrt; her father, Henry Sehrt; her brother, Edward H. Sehrt, and Miss Cecilia Schane; 3702 Dillon street, a teacher at the Highlandtown public school, are all in Berlin. Edward H. Sehrt has been a student at the University of Leipzig for more than a year. He was visited there by his father and sister, and because of the war trouble decided to return to this country with them.

RAILROADS INCREASE

Baltimore Sun
early September 1914

99

DR. EDWARD HENRY SEHRT,

98, the chairman of the department of Germanic languages and literatures at George Washington University from 1926 until he retired in 1953 with the rank of professor emeritus, died Nov. 20 at the Manor Care nursing home in Arlington. He had congestive heart failure and respiratory ailments.

Dr. Sehrt, who lived in McLean, was a specialist in Germanic linguistics and philology. He was an authority on the works of Notker the German of St. Gall, Switzerland, who flourished about 1000 A.D. He wrote numerous articles and books on these and related topics.

A native of Highlandtown in Baltimore, Dr. Sehrt graduated from Johns Hopkins University in 1911 and took his doctorate in German there in 1915.

He taught at Bryn Mawr College in Bryn Mawr, Pa., and Washington College in Chestertown, Md., and then returned to Johns Hopkins as a research fellow from 1920 to 1922. He taught at Gettysburg College until he joined the faculty of George Washington University in 1926.

Dr. Sehrt was a member of the Modern Languages Association of America, the Linguistics Society of America, the Medieval Academy of America and the Baltimore Chapter of the Goethe Society.

His first wife, the former Cecilia Shane, died in 1960. Their daughter, Cecilia Sehrt, died in 1928.

Dr. Sehrt's survivors include his wife, Helen Ludwig Sehrt of McLean; one sister, Lula Cameron of Gaithersburg, and one brother, Charles G. Sehrt of Baltimore.

Mrs. Henry Sehrt.

At her home in Baltimore, Md., this morning at an early hour, Mrs. Henry Sehrt passed away at the age of 71 years. She suffered a fall on Thursday last, and was apparently recovering nicely, when her death came as a sudden shock.

Mrs. Sehrt, previous to her marriage, was Miss Caroline Baker, and she was born and reared in Baltimore. Besides her husband, three children survive: Dr. Edward Sehrt, Professor in the Department of Romance Languages in George Washington University; Charles Sehrt, a business man of Baltimore; and Mrs. Norman W. Cameron, of West Chester. There are four grandchildren.

SEHRT.—On May 9, 1929, CAROLINE (nee Becker), aged 71 years, beloved wife of Henry Sehrt. Funeral from her late residence, 2925 Overland avenue, on Monday afternoon at 2 o'clock. Interment in London Park Cemetery.
13e

100

$144,423 IS LEFT
BY HENRY SEHRT

Inventory Of East End Grocer's Estate Is Filed In Orphans' Court

Property Includes Stocks And Other Securities Valued At $129,423

Henry Sehrt, who operated a grocery at 3421 Eastern avenue, left an estate of $144,423, according to an inventory filed yesterday in Orphans' Court.

Stocks, bonds and other securities made up $129,423 of the property, the remainder in debts due the estate, according to the inventory. Mr. Sehrt, who died November 5, left all his property to his three children.

Securities Listed

Security holdings included:

BONDS

City of Hagerstown	$5,322
State Roads	2,100
Anne Arundel county	8,200
Annapolis Incinerator	3,300
Baltimore county	9,220
Baltimore city	6,610
State of Maryland	6,300
Associated Gas and Electric Company	3,930
Cumberland General Improvement	2,300

STOCKS

Twelve shares Chrysler Corporation common	1,020
Thirty-six shares American X Gas and Electric common	1,404
Commercial Credit Company	3,693
Forty-one shares Electric Bond and Share preferred	2,501

Certificates Included

Mr. Sehrt also held $3,000 worth of certificates of deposit and $350 in voting trust certificates, the inventory showed.

The children who will share the estate are: Charles G. Sehrt, Edward H. Sehrt and Mrs. Lulu M. Cameron. Charles Sehrt, who lives at 2401 Mayfield avenue, is executor of his father's will.

HENRY SEHRT

........DEALER IN........

GENERAL MERCHANDISE

3421-23-25 EASTERN AVENUE, Highlandtown

BALTIMORE. MD.

WINES AND LIQUORS
FOR FAMILY USE

PAINTS, HARDWARE,
GLASS AND
BUILDERS' SUPPLIES

Know All Men by these Presents: That I, Henry Sehrt, in consideration of the sum of Eight Thousand ($8,000.00) Dollars do hereby sell and transfer to my son, Charles G. Sehrt, the business heretofore conducted by me at 3421-23-25 Eastern Ave. together with the stock of merchandise and fixtures etc. contained in the stores, cellars and outbuildings; and also the right to conduct the business in my name; and subject to such rental for the use of the premises as may be agreed upon by the parties aforesaid. The purchase price to be payable at such times and in such amounts as may be agreeable to my son; the date and amount of each payment to be noted hereon.

Witness my hand and seal this *first* day of *January*, *1917*

(SEAL)

Hy Sehrt

Test:

Caroline Sehrt

1917 June 13,	1,500.00	—	Hy Sehrt
Aug 8,	1,500.00	—	Hy Sehrt
Nov 15,	1,000.00	—	Hy Sehrt
1918 Feb 20,	1,000.00	—	Hy Sehrt
Mch 6,	500.00	—	Hy Sehrt
April 10	2500.00	—	Hy Sehrt
	8000.00		

Particular Attention Paid To Orders

BRoadway 6-9205

Baltimore-24, Md., _____ 19___

M_____

To HENRY SEHRT, Dr.

... DEALER IN ...

GROCERIES. KITCHEN UTENSILS. PAINTS. OILS. GLASS. BRUSHES.
HARDWARE. ETC.

3421-3423-3425 EASTERN AVENUE

Betty Sehrt—1918
1 year old

1918—Papa Cooley with Betty Sehrt

August 11, 1920
Wedding of Lula Sehrt and Norman Cameron
Flower girls
(L) Cecelia Sehrt (R) Betty Sehrt

Sehrt family gathering—Circa 1923
Standing (L to R)
Henry, Lula, Caroline, Mabel, Ed, Cecelia
Sitting
Charles (Pop), Caroline Cameron, Betty, Little Cecelia,
Mary Louise (Snooky) and Norman Cameron (Jr.)

1946—Uncle Ed, Aunt Lula, Pop

5 Sehrt grandchildren
Cecilia & Betty in back. Mary Louise, Norman, Caroline in front.
Circa 1924

Henry Sehrt holding grand daughter, Mary Louise

Poor copy of Sehrt family photo Charles behind Mabel
on left, Henry and Caroline, Ed behind Cecilia, Betty
& Cecilia—little girls in front c. 1920–21

Home of Henry & Caroline Sehrt at Harford
Road, Baltimore & Overland Road

20

Professors Wolfram K. Legner and James C. King, of the German Department, present a Festschrift honoring the 80th birthday of Professor Emeritus Edward Henry Sehrt.

ABOUT PROFESSOR SEHRT

Edward H. Sehrt, whose 80th birthday on March 3, 1968, occasioned this article, as well as the *Festschrift* volume he is reading here, was Professor of German and Chairman of the Department of Germanic Languages and Literatures at The George Washington University from 1926 to 1953. Earlier he taught at the University of Delaware, Bryn Mawr College, Washington College, and Gettysburg College. He is a graduate of Johns Hopkins University. A.B. 1911 and Ph.D. 1915, where he pursued Germanic and Indo-European studies.

Among Professor Sehrt's publications are the dictionaries *Vollständiges Wörterbuch zum Heliand und zur altsächsischen Genesis* (Göttingen: Vandenhoeck & Ruprecht, 1925), *Notker-Wortschatz* (Halle: Max Niemeyer Verlag, 1955), and *Notker-Glossar* (Tübingen: Max Niemeyer Verlag, 1962). With Professor Emeritus Taylor Starck, of Harvard University, he began a new, critical edition of the works of the Old High German writer Notker Teutonicus—*Notkers des Deutschen Werke*, published in the series *Altdeutsche Textbibliothek* (Halle: Max Niemeyer Verlag, 1933-35, 1952-55). His research and writing continue undiminished.

Few scholars succeed as completely as Professor Sehrt in achieving a balance between research and teaching. On the graduate level he taught general linguistics, Sanskrit, comparative Germanic grammar, Gothic, Old Norse, Old English, Old High German, and Middle High German. His undergraduate courses included German classicism and romanticism, Goethe's *Faust*, and the drama. Throughout his career he also delighted in teaching beginning and intermediate German.

1947. Mayfield Avenue—Thankgiving?
Back Row (L to R)—Dr. Edward Sehrt, Cousin Harry Baker, Bill Parks, Mary Louise Parks, Betty Sehrt, Charles Sehrt (Pop), Dr. Norman Cameron, Sr.
Middle—Cousin Margaret Baker, Aunt Hula Cameron, Mabel Sehrt, Mrs. Baker, Aunt Cecelia Sehrt
Front—Aunt Eva Baker, Charles King Markline

MRS. MARIAN DOBLER BROOKE
1343 Emory Road
Atlanta, GA 30306
(404) 378-1612

One of mother's best friends growing up

****

Editor, *Baltimore Sun*
501 N. Calvert St.
Baltimore, MD 21278

Dear Editor:

A friend sent me the article on Mayfield that appeared in
the Jan. 7, 1990 issue of the *Baltimore Sun*. She knew that
I had lived in Mayfield years ago. Indeed I did, and would
like to fill in some material that may of use to you in the
future.

Mayfield was developed by my grandfather, Judge John J.
Dobler of the Baltimore Supreme Court. He must have
purchased the land around 1910 and built his home at 2224
Mayfield Avenue a couple of years later. The bricks of his
home were made in Annapolis and are the same color as those
used in the Naval Academy's buildings. The lot is
exceptionally wide for a city residence. The home was sold
around 1925 to the Phelps who owned it until a few years
ago.

The city wanted to name Mayfield Avenue for Judge Dobler but
he declined the offer. Instead the city named a short
street between Harford and Montebello Drive as Dobler
Avenue.

I found the enclosed clippings concerning Erdman Avenue in
my grandfather's scrapbook. He offers to grade Erdman Avenue
from Harford to Belair Road and to improve the sidewalk.

I was born in the house at 3309 Crossland Avenue which my
father, John S. Dobler, built a year or two before. One of
my childhood interests was to watch the construction of all
of the houses pictured in your article and many of the
streets in Mayfield.

Sincerely yours,

Marian D. Brooke
Marian D. Brooke

Copy: Dr. Michele Le Faivre
      Mr. George M. Marsalek
      Ms. Mary E. Medland

2401 was between the cross streets of Norman and Crossland Avenues

Pop bought 2401 property from Judge Dobler in 1923 and house was finished in 1924 —

110

Judge Dobler Makes Liberal Offer To The City.

The Commissioners for Opening Streets have received a letter from Judge John J. Dobler offering to pay for the grading of Erdman avenue, from the Harford road to the Belair road, and also to improve the sidewalks along this avenue, provided the city will pay for any readjustment of water mains that may be necessary, and also provided the city will pave the avenue.

The Commissioners refer to the proposition as a most public-spirited one, and they are heartily in favor of accepting it. The cost, it is said, will be about the same to each party. A conference will be held with Mayor Timanus tomorrow morning at 11 o'clock to decide what will be done.

In his letter Judge Dobler said:

Erdman avenue from the Harford road to the Belair road has never been physically graded or paved. From the Harford road eastwardly 1550 feet the grade is about to be re-established. On the northwest side of the avenue from the Clifton Park gate several lots are about to be improved by the erection of valuable buildings.

If your Commission will pave the avenue from the Park gate to the Harford road with the most approved macadam pavement 26 feet wide (there being no necessity for a sidewalk on the Park side), I will pay the entire cost of grading the avenue from the Park gate to the Harford road and will improve the northwest sidewalk by a concrete pavement four feet wide, work to be done under the supervision of the City Engineer, the city, however, to provide for any adjustment of its water mains.

An offer to deed the bed of Belle avenue east from Garrison avenue and south to Kate avenue to the city was unconditionally accepted today by the Commissioners for Opening Streets. City Solicitor Bruce has been requested to have the deed drawn up. The offer was made by Messrs. James E. Ingram and William L. Stanabury, joint owners of the bed of the street.

sweep the ground. Over the top is on, extending back to the cross-piece

"*Catching or bagging.*—There a for this purpose. The cheapest to bag the insects. A frame two ing as it is to be drawn by men ing behind and ending in a sma and two or three feet long, with light and permit the dumping of insects gravitate toward the win full they may be emptied into a machines will prove most ser kerosene pans, just described, by having runners at distances or so in front of the mouth, so a

JUDGE DOBLER'S OFFER TO CITY

Will Grade Erdman Avenue and Improve Sidewalks If Water Mains Are Readjusted.

Judge John J. Dobler has written to the Commissioners for Opening streets offering to pay for the grading of Erdman avenue, from the Harford road to the Belair road, and also improve the sidewalks along the avenue, if the city will pay for the readjustment of water mains. The Commissioners are in favor of accepting the offer, and will confer with Mayor Timanus this morning in regard to it. Judge Dobler said in his letter to the Commissioners:

Erdman avenue, from the Harford road to the Belair road, has never been physically graded or paved. From the Harford road eastwardly 1,550 feet the grade is about to be re-established. On the northwest side of the avenue from the Clifton Park gate several lots are about to be improved by the erection of valuable buildings.

If your commission will pave the avenue from the park gate to the Harford road with the most approved macadam pavement 26 feet wide (there being no necessity for a sidewalk on the park side), I will pay the entire cost of grading the avenue from the park gate to the Harford road and will improve the northwest sidewalk by a concrete pavement four feet wide, work to be done under the supervision of the City Engineer, the city, however, to provide for any adjustment of its water mains.

The Commissioners have

ARNVOIR IS SOLD FOR DEVELOPMENT

Fine Place On The Harford Road Was Occupied By Judge Dobler.

Arnvoir, on Harford avenue, for the last nine years the home of Judge John J. Dobler of the Supreme Bench, was sold today by the owner of the property, James A. Clarke, a prominent grain merchant of Baltimore, to Dr. Theodore Cooke. Dr. Cooke will probably develop the tract in conjunction with some property he owns adjoining it.

Arnvoir consists of about four acres of land, and is located on the west side of the Harford road, opposite Clifton Park. The purchasing price is withheld, but it is understood to have been in the neighborhood of $35,000.

The property at one time was owned by the late Thomas Kelso, and there is an old mansion on the place. Mr. Clark bought the place about 10 years ago, and about nine years ago Judge Dobler leased it.

Dr. Cooke, the purchaser, has owned a large tract of land in the rear of the property just bought for some time. Arnvoir, however, cut the former property off from the main avenue, and in der to get an outlet Mr. Clark's property was bought. Dr. Cooke now has a tage on Harford avenue of about eet.

2401 MAYFIELD AVENUE
BALTIMORE, MD.

11/29/45

Dear Folks:-

So glad to get the good news (although we are a little slow saying so), Elizabeth had called Betty as soon as she had received the news. We are all so happy, that you have such a dear baby girl, we wouldn't want our baby to be any other than the dear boy he is, but I know Betty envies every one of her friends who has a baby girl, she says you just can't dress up a boy in poke bonnets and pinafores.

Am sure Marian is back home by the time this letter is received, and we do hope she will gain her strength rapidly, so she can have

Note: Copy of letter written by Michel Sehrt (11/29/1945)
It was sent to Mother by her friend Marianne Dohler

I've been looking through a box of "memories" & about this week this an Wednesday. Thank you so much — hope I see my pink eight. (this was on my pink eight)

112

health and strength to take care of
her dear family. Do wish we were
nearer, so we could drop in and
do little things for you.

Betty called Mignon & Naomi Zelle's
mother was in the store, so told her.

Am enclosing 2 newspaper articles
I thought you would enjoy reading.

We've had the most horrible rainy
weather since Sunday - 2.2 inches of
rain - lucky it hasn't been snow!
so we'd be snowed in. Charles hasn't
been out of the house since Sunday
and he driving us all nearly crazy,
so much energy. Both girls are
down town today. I was shopping.
I had to put him to bed before writing
you. Just can't write letters when he
is around. he always wants paper and
a pencil to write to his Daddy to tell

"Charles" (Charles K. Markline, Sr.) is 2½ yrs. old at
this time

(3)

2401 MAYFIELD AVENUE
BALTIMORE, MD.

him to come home. Today he removed
the fire screen from the fire place,
said Santa Claus couldn't get out
of the chimney.

Saw Mr. Dotter several times
driving by, he looks very well.
Window shades are all even and
I know he is a good house keeper.

The Xmas rush at the store is on,
but with no soap powder, eggs, very
little butter, no candy, nuts limited
about all one can say is "no, sorry."
Guess there won't be many Xmas
turkies this year.

We'll call your family and keep
posted on the latest news. Only
wish we lived nearer, we'd love

→ Check this paragraph— WW II had been
over three months before

114

to see you.

Betty thinks and talks about Marian so often, too bad they must live so far away.

Best wishes for a quick recovery to your former pep, Marian, and I hope your mother holds out, these Grand-mothers take child care so seriously, even after they were successful in raising their own.

Tommy and Charles would have a grand time together at X'mas time. Our love to you all —

Sincerely,
Mabel Schut

These evening

Classified
GE 10N

Real Estate

Mayfield residents love it and don't want to leave it

Families moving up try to stay in area

By Mary E. Medland
Special to The Sun

When a Mayfield family wants to move to a bigger house, they will usually try to find one in Mayfield itself.

That's a good indication of how the residents feel about their neighborhood.

Bordered by Lake Montebello Drive and Chesterfield, Crossland

NEIGHBORHOOD PROFILE

and Erdman avenues, Mayfield is lapped by Herring Run Park, Clifton Park Golf Course, and Lake Montebello.

The 1980 census listed the population as slightly more than 1,000 in 398 households.

Mayfield has always been a comfortable family enclave, a stable neighborhood with a variety of styles and sizes of houses.

Housing prices are currently low, but are steadily rising because of the neighborhood's affordability and housing values and its location only minutes from downtown.

The houses are a mix of detached and semi-detached. The individual houses usually are brick and stone though there are some frame cottages. For the most part, the semi-detached houses are brick.

About nine houses were sold last year, and the prices ranged from the mid-$80,000s up to $150,000.

Melvin Knight, a real estate agent with Chase Fitzgerald, describes a

house he sold last year.

"It had four bedrooms, a finishe basement with a fireplace, living an

See **MAYFIELD**, 2N, Col.

THE SUN/WALTER M. McCARDELL
Homes on Crossland Avenue show the differing styles that are a feature of Mayfield.

Housing is still a good investment despite pessimist

When Mayfield families want to move

MAYFIELD, from 1N

dining rooms, a kitchen, 2½ baths, a garage. The lot was about 25 by 90, and the house had 3,200 plus feet. It sold for $84,000. The new owners put in a new kitchen."

Mr. Knight says now it could be sold for $115,000 because of the new kitchen and the rising prices for homes in the area. A comparable house in Stoneleigh would sell for $140,000 and a similar one in Roland Park for $180,000, he says.

There are rarely more than three to four houses for sale in Mayfield at any given time, he notes.

People seem to move up within the neighborhood — leaving a small house, but not the neighborhood, for a larger one, Mr. Knight says. The family that put in the new kitchen is already thinking of trading up in Mayfield, he adds.

Mrs. Frances Gast, a real estate agent with O'Connor, Piper, & Flynn, who grew up in Mayfield and still lives there, says that a house with three large bedrooms, 1½ to two baths, a detached garage and a fin-

ished family room sells for about $100,000.

"It is an area that is just now becoming hot," she says.

A documented early history of Mayfield is elusive. Some believe it dates back to the turn of the century though some homes were still being built there in the 1950s.

Michele LeFaivre, professor of architecture and urban design at the Johns Hopkins School of Continuing Studies and a planning consultant, says she believes the area was developed by one person in the 1910s and early 1920s.

Many residents believe that the area's development, although undocumented, was tied in with the plans for Herring Run Park, which was a part of the parks and green space planning in Baltimore by the Olmsted brothers, Frederick Law and John Charles, who were renowned 19th-century landscape architects.

Dr. LeFaivre maintains that the best quality home construction in the city was in houses built in the 1920s. And Mayfield is known for some of the best architecture in the

city, she said. She likes the good de tail and the durability of Mayfield' homes along with the careful atter tion to green spaces that reflect th "garden suburb" movement planned development that originate in England in the 1900s.

Dr. LeFaivre also notes that an other aim of the garden subur movement that can be seen in May field was to create medium-densit neighborhoods.

Residents are protective of th neighborhood. Kenneth Marsalek, longtime resident who is known a Mayfield's historian, points to tw zoning clashes the Mayfield Improv ment Association got involved in.

The Baurenschmidts — a famil of prominent local brewers — ha its home at the corner of Erdma and Harford Roads in Mayfield. Se eral years ago the house was in th process of being sold to an undertal er for his business when the commu nity association heard about thes plans. After the headline "Undertal ers Out to Bury Mayfield" appeare in the community newsletter, res dents raised an outcry, and the plar

ip, they try to stay in the neighborhood

were changed. The house was sold in 1980 for $66,000 as a private residence.

Another zoning clash concerned a local drugstore that requested a liquor license. Residents fought against the license, and ultimately the city liquor board denied the request.

Mike Ciuchta, president of the Mayfield Improvement Association, founded in the 1930s, has warm praise for the neighborhood. He attributes some of its stability to the fact that 95 percent of the houses are owner-occupied.

In the late 1970s, the area was zoned R-1 which means that none of the houses can be turned into multifamily dwellings. The multifamily houses that were already in existence were grandfathered in.

"The crime rate here is very low," Mr. Ciuchta adds, "probably because it is such a close-knit neighborhood, with an effective block watch program."

One question that concerns Mr. Ciuchta is the future of Memorial Stadium, which is within easy walking distance. An association member has met with representatives of the Memorial Stadium Reuse Task Force, set up to look at the options for the site when the Orioles move to the new stadium. Virtually everyone acknowledges that the neighborhood will be affected by what is done with the stadium site.

The task force report is due to be completed this spring, according to Rachel Edds, assistant director of the Baltimore City Department of Planning.

Ms. Edds, incidentally, points out another advantage of Mayfield. "There is no through traffic, yet the neighborhood is within easy access to the major arteries, it is 10 minutes from downtown, and bus lines are easily available," she says.

Mrs. Gast notes that the neighborhood always seems to have a good mix of people — from young to old.

In the winter houses are decorated for Christmas, and the winner of the neighborhood association light-

ing contest gets to choose a charity to receive a donation. In the summer there's a block party, and a fundraiser at Halloween.

THE SUN/WALTER M. McCAHDELL JR.

These brick homes show the quality typical in the neighborhood.

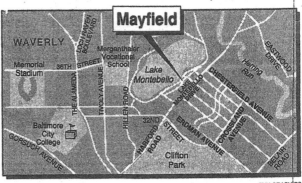

SUN GRAPHICS

Markline, Charles K

From: Camloch@aol.com
Sent: Tuesday, March 23, 1999 6:05 PM
To: Charles.k.markline@lmco.com
Subject: Contact with long lost cousin

Dear Charles,

When I found your e-mail today, I thought it was in response to the packet of stuff I sent you on Saturday. However, it appeared as I continued to read, that you just wrote of your own accord. I am still so dumb about the Internet that I don't know how to find people's on-line addresses as you do telephone numbers in a directory. Anyhow, it was good to hear from you and to read about your family. You seem to have anticipated the questions I posed in my letter to you.

I am impressed with all the degrees in your family! A very learned group. Let's see - no doctorates in our immediate family.. I have a masters in Liberal Arts from Johns Hopkins, Bruce has an MBA from Harvard, and Alex has a Masters in broadcast journalism from New York Univ. Chip, who is the most brilliant of my children, and the most scholarly, has never wanted to get a graduate degree.
You say that you teach as a hobby at Chapman Univ. and Univ. of S.F. but you don't say what subject(s) you teach. I am happy to learn that you will soon have a grandchild. They are a great joy.

Write again after you receive the packet I sent and we can talk about genealogy and what info or documents we need to exchange. I have amassed a tremendous amount of information about the Camerons and the Northups (my family) since I became interested in the 1960's, but I have not put it into very readable order. There is just so much time I can spend immersed in libraries and at the computer. Then I feel the need to get out and be with people!

Isn't e-mail the greatest?!

Cordially, ROLDAH

Mrs. Norman W. Cameron, Jr.
15 Brook Court
Summit, New Jersey 07901

Dec. 2

Dear Betty & Charles,

In case Caroline hasn't notified you, you may want to know that your Aunt Leila died on November 28 at the Asbury Village health care center in Gaithersburg. We buried her yesterday in Loudon Park Cemetery in the Sehrt plot. Another cold winter day and a remarkable seventh November family death. Lula failed rapidly in the last year and her body just wore out it seems.

We are all well and plodding away at assorted jobs. Ross will be leaving the family sphere next month as he moves to California to accept a job with a newspaper in Pleasanton, near San Francisco. In case you are wondering, he is a "photo-journalist" — newspaper photographer, that is.

Hope your family is happy and healthy. Best wishes for 1990

Cordially,
Roedah

120

Markline, Charles K

From: Finisterre@aol.com
Sent: Monday, March 22, 1999 1:09 PM
To: charles.k.markline@lmco.com
Subject: Sehrt family

Dear Charlie,

I've forwarded your address to my mother, who was very upset to learn that your aunt had neglected to pass along the Sehrt family information that my mother had entrusted to her. She was so upset, in fact, that the last time I spoke to her she was making an attempt to collate all her Sehrt stuff once again and said she hoped to send it on to you "real soon." I told her what you'd told me 'bout the papers and photographs you own and I quoted at length from your email; she said "I knew all that stuff" about the Sehrts -- referring, in part no doubt, to my grandmother's getting trapped behind German lines at the start of WWI. (It was news to me, though.) Still I know that she'd be very glad to hear from you. And she's a much more faithful and informative correspondent than I am.

Caroline and Tom's address is

> Mr. & Mrs. Thomas J. Hendrickson
> 65 Confederate Drive
> Gettysburg, PA 17325
> thomasjh@mail.cvn.net

I suspect that they'd be pleased to get a note from you, though they're not as good about answering as they were a couple years ago.

Hope you've had some luck reaching Ross. I've written to him twice in the past couple weeks and I have yet to get a word in reply.

Chip

From:	Finisterre@aol.com
Sent:	Friday, March 12, 1999 2:32 PM
To:	charles.k.markline@lmco.com
Subject:	Yesteryear & now

Dear Charlie,

Memory's a funny thing, and mine's not very good... about the thing's that've happened to me. (I remember things I read though fairly well.) I've often thought, in that regard, that I resemble Lula Sehrt, who didn't seem to dwell much in the past but looked forward or sideways instead: for whom the past was in many ways dead. So if I've mis-remembered, or misconstrued, what you describe as a closer relationship between the members of the Sehrt family I'm not all that surprised. You're also I think a little older than I am (I'm 46) and probably saw some more of them -- of Charles and Ed, and certainly of my grandfather, Norman, who died a good five years 'fore I was born. To be honest with you, I can't even visualize Mabel, who must've died when I was barely out of diapers. The wife that I remember (fairly well) was Charles's second wife Kay, whom he married when I think I was eight. Her name before she married him was Kraft, and she had a daughter who died of cancer just before, or maybe after, they were wed. I can still recall descriptions of her agony and how the morphine wouldn't dull it towards the end.

Caroline and her husband, Tom, are doing fine. In fact I saw them just a week ago, when they were here in New York on a "cultural" tour. (They went to see a play, a concert and a couple of museums.) Both of them, of course, have been retired for quite a while. She's nearing 77, he's a year younger, but both of them are well and even flourishing. When my grandmother died, the bulk of her estate devolved on Caroline; I can't recall how much, but probably 85 per cent of it at least -- and in the past ten years this has freed them from a host of constraints and allowed them to travel a good deal. Already this year I think they've been abroad twice: once for several weeks to visit friends and old relationships in France and once, for close to a month, on a cruise through the "Spice Islands," the former Moluccas (Indonesia mostly -- I forget what else).

As for my brother Ross, the one who lives in Pleasanton, he works as a newspaper photographer for the Heyward... Daily Advance? I think it's called "The Advance" but the last time I asked him flat out he never bothered to respond. He's 38 and lives alone but has a girlfriend who's also a journalist, a reporter for the Oakland Tribune... or whatever that newspaper's called. You could always try to reach him at his home (see below) or, if you'd rather, via email, at drosscameron@msn.com. He almost never responds to my phone calls or email; you may have better luck. Here's his address:

> D. Ross Cameron
> 7670-F Canyon Meadows Circle
> Pleasanton, CA 94588
> (510) 734-8655

His area code may have changed, but 510 is what it was a couple years ago.

My mother hasn't worked on the Sehrt (...Cameron/Northup) family tree in the past couple years with the passion that she had for it once. Or that, at least, is my impression. But she is nothing, my mom, if not organized, and she's got tons of stuff around that she collected in the '60s, '70s and '80s, including photographs, letters, chronologies and a couple family Bibles. Most of this she's catalogued and digested and transcribed and has no trouble recollecting. Some of it, indeed, she claims she's even sent to you. "A while back," she wrote me, "Mary Louise told me Charles was interested in the Sehrt genealogy so I took the time to get a lot of it together and write up everything I knew for him. I sent it to him but never heard a word in return." Did the stuff ever reach you? It sounds as though it may've gotten lost. I know that she'd be interested in whatever information you've amassed, and I'm sure that in return she'd be happy to furnish you with whatever information she dug up for you before.

Glad to get details about your mom. If you think she'd be interested in writing to my mom, give her the following address (which I suspect she already has; it hasn't changed in years):

    Roldah Cameron
    15 Brook Court
    Summit, NJ 07901
    camloch@aol.com

And give me yours, why don't you, so I can pass it along to my mom?

Hope you're doing well,
Chip

Markline, Charles K

From: Finisterre@aol.com
Sent: Wednesday, March 10, 1999 2:51 PM
To: charles.k.markline@lmco.com
Subject: Cameron family (w/ emphasis on Roldah)

Dear Charlie,

Thanks for bringing me up to date, or briefing me at least on your family and you and also, I should say, for un-deluding me. I knew your mother and your aunt by their Christian names: as Cousin Betty and Cousin Mary Louise. Last names, at that age, had a way of eluding me -- as they do indeed increasingly at this.

I was sorry to hear about your aunt, very sorry and sad -- though once you mentioned that she'd died I had the vaguest recollection someone'd told me. We'd been out of touch for years; I'm not sure why -- no doubt because my father died, in 1982, and severed in the process the only meaningful, the only integral link between our never-very-intimate two broods. After that, and probably for a long time before it, my only point of contact with her family was the Christmas card that I believe she sent my mother every year, and after moving to New York I rarely heard about those in detail.

My mother's still alive and doing well; after a short-lived, and disastrous, second marriage (it lasted less than a year), she's resigned herself to living in New Jersey, by herself, in the house that she built in the year or two that followed my father's death. But she works, at least a part of the time, and she travels some. She's also fond of the opera and of music, and sometimes gets to New York to see plays, especially since my wife (who's an actress) sometimes plays in them herself. She's down in Florida at the moment, visiting friends of ours from Baltimore (from the olde days) and gets around a fair amount; last year, for example, she traveled out to Omaha and to Oklahoma City (where one of my brothers lives), spent a portion of the month of August in Santa Fe and travelled back and forth to Delaware, to the seashore, where she still owns a cottage in Rehoboth. Now and again, though not every year, she even gets as far as San Francisco. I have another brother there, in Pleasanton, in the Silicon Valley.

How's your mother doing? I asked my mom what she could tell me about her but she said your mother doesn't write her very much, or that she isn't that forthcoming when she does. I hope she's well and that you'll give her my regards... that you'll remember me to her and tell her how fondly I think about our meetings years ago when we were young.

Regards and best wishes,
Chip

George Percival Scriven:
An American in Bohol, The Philippines, 1899-1901

An On-line Archival Collection
Special Collections Library, Duke University

The U.S. Military Occupation of Bohol

1900-1902

by Norman Cameron

Bio - Info on Norman Dr. Cameron

In what follows I've referred to "my grandfather" and to things that he wrote in a diary he kept, and I should probably explain who he was.

The Spaniards had sent friars; the Americans sent teachers. And they didn't waste time: they sent seven or eight hundred in the first year alone (1901-1902). The majority of these men and women - some with teaching experience, some without - came across on a steamer called the "Thomas"; my grandfather, then twenty-six, was one of them. His name, like mine, was Norman Cameron. After graduating from college in 1895, he had taught for six years in the public schools in Blacksburg, South Carolina, but up until 1901 he had never been west of the Allegheny mountains. In the Philippines, where he arrived aboard the "Thomas" in August 1901, he was assigned to teach school at Tagbilaran, Bohol. The war was still in progress when he got there and culminated just a couple of months later (on Bohol, that is). He remained at Tagbilaran till 1904, when he was reassigned briefly to the grade school at Tubigon. Throughout his sojourn on the island he kept a diary, which, though it runs to five volumes and covers two hundred pages in typescript, grows increasingly perfunctory as time goes on and as the novelty of his surroundings began to wear off. In March 1904, he left the Philippines, discontented and disillusioned by the fights that he'd had with the Bureau of Education in the islands. Back in the United States, he resumed his career, first at the Kalamazoo Teachers College in Kalamazoo, Michigan and later at the West Chester Normal School (now West Chester State University) in West Chester, PA. Somewhere along the line he acquired a Ph.D. at the University of Pennsylvania. While serving as the principal of the Baltimore Teachers Training School, in 1920, he met and married my grandmother, a 26-year old teacher trainee named Lula Sehrt. In 1928, he returned to the West Chester Normal School (with his wife and two children) and remained there as president for the next eight years, when he was ousted from the place for political reasons. He ended his career as superintendent of schools for the Garfield (New Jersey) public school system (1936-1941). In 1947, without warning, he died of a heart attack in Towson, Maryland. He was 72 years old.

From the sound of it, the island of Bohol was one of the last places in the world that you *wouldn't* want to invade. From a sightseer's point of view, certainly, it had everything -- had there been any sightseers: beautiful weather, beautiful beaches, interesting and ornamental old churches, a sparkling sea. It even had souvenirs: native mats and straw hats and exotic fruit. Its people were picturesque too, a handsome, hard-working, placable folk who were sometimes known as the "Chinamen of the Philippines," in part because they were (many of them) ethnic Chinese -- but also because their industry and their skill as traders were a source of envy. In 1898 the island had become its own country, and the people of Bohol had governed it with tact and moderation and shown a broad-backed self-reliance in rebuffing an invasion from Cebu. It was the sort of place that could make you wistful. And "Indeed," confessed George Scriven, thinking back, "if I were ever tempted to play Robinson Crusoe Bohol would be my island." All that was missing really, from a sightseer's point of view, was hard currency. All that was missing was an American owner.

125

From: Finisterre@aol.com
Sent: Friday, March 12, 1999 2:32 PM
To: charles.k.markline@lmco.com
Subject: Yesteryear & now

Dear Charlie,

Memory's a funny thing, and mine's not very good... about the thing's that've happened to me. (I remember things I read though fairly well.) I've often thought, in that regard, that I resemble Lula Sehrt, who didn't seem to dwell much in the past but looked forward or sideways instead: for whom the past was in many ways dead. So if I've mis-remembered, or misconstrued, what you describe as a closer relationship between the members of the Sehrt family I'm not all that surprised. You're also I think a little older than I am (I'm 46) and probably saw some more of them -- of Charles and Ed, and certainly of my grandfather, Norman, who died a good five years 'fore I was born. To be honest with you, I can't even visualize Mabel, who must've died when I was barely out of diapers. The wife that I remember (fairly well) was Charles's second wife Kay, whom she married when I think I was eight. Her name before she married him was Kraft, and she had a daughter who died of cancer just before, or maybe after, they were wed. I can still recall descriptions of her agony and how the morphine wouldn't dull it towards the end.

Caroline and her husband, Tom, are doing fine. In fact I saw them just a week ago, when they were here in New York on a "cultural" tour. (They went to see a play, a concert and a couple of museums.) Both of them, of course, have been retired for quite a while. She's nearing 77, he's a year younger, but both of them are well and even flourishing. When my grandmother died, the bulk of her estate devolved on Caroline; I can't recall how much, but probably 85 per cent of it at least -- and in the past ten years this has freed them from a host of constraints and allowed them to travel a good deal. Already this year I think they've been abroad twice: once for several weeks to visit friends and old relationships in France and once, for close to a month, on a cruise through the "Spice Islands," the former Moluccas (Indonesia mostly -- I forget what else).

As for my brother Ross, the one who lives in Pleasanton, he works as a newspaper photographer for the Heyward... Daily Advance? I think it's called "The Advance" but the last time I asked him flat out he never bothered to respond. He's 38 and lives alone but has a girlfriend who's also a journalist, a reporter for the Oakland Tribune... or whatever that newspaper's called. You could always try to reach him at his home (see below) or, if you'd rather, via email, at drosscameron@msn.com. He almost never responds to my phone calls or email; you may have better luck. Here's his address:

> D. Ross Cameron
> 7670-F Canyon Meadows Circle
> Pleasanton, CA 94588
> (510) 734-8655

His area code may have changed, but 510 is what it was a couple years ago.

My mother hasn't worked on the Sehrt (...Cameron/Northup) family tree in the past couple years with the passion that she had for it once. Or that, at least, is my impression. But she is nothing, my mom, if not organized, and she's got tons of stuff around that she collected in the '60s, '70s and '80s, including photographs, letters, chronologies and a couple family Bibles. Most of this she's catalogued and digested and transcribed and has no trouble recollecting. Some of it, indeed, she claims she's even sent to you. "A while back," she wrote me, "Mary Louise told me Charles was interested in the Sehrt genealogy so I took the time to get a lot of it together and write up everything I knew for him. I sent it to him but never heard a word in return." Did the stuff ever reach you? It sounds as though it may've gotten lost. I know that she'd be interested in whatever information you've amassed, and I'm sure that in return she'd be happy to furnish you with whatever information she dug up for you before.

Baker Chronicles

BAECKER - name later spelled BECKER and then BAKER

Attempts to pinpoint when Henry Baecker arrived in the USA have been unsuccessful thus far. I have been to the National Archives, Maryland Historical Society and Hall of Records in Annapolis to do research.* At the National Archives immigration lists for Baltimore in the period 1840-1855 reveal at least 21 Heinrich Baeckers or Beckers, but none of them seemed right for one reason or another. e.g. On the Federal list there is a Heinrich Baecker, age 29, who arrived port of Baltimore on 6 May 1852 on ship Bremerhaven (H-96-198 74). His destination was Baltimore (many immigrants were headed for places farther inland or south) and his occupation "tailor". Right name, right age, right destination, wrong occupation. Our Henry Baecker made his living as a cabinetmaker. Maybe Henry changed his mind about how to earn a living after he arrived here? Doubtful.

Henry's death certificate states that at the time of his death in 1890 he had been a resident of the city of Baltimore for 41 years which would mean he came there in 1849. Therefore, rule out H. Baecker above. But wait! Info on a death certificate is given by a survivor who may not have all the facts.

Death certificates and census reports agree that both Henry and his wife, Louisa, were born in Germany (family tradition says from the Black Forest area), but no one knows when or where they were married. Uncle Ed thought they were married before they came to the US. Lula thought that Henry came here first and then sent for Louisa. If so, you'd think I could find a record of her arrival, but I haven't found any Louisa Becker in the records. Of course, I'm looking for the wrong name if they weren't married until she got here. Even her daughter, Caroline Sehrt, did not know her mother's maiden name when asked to give it for Louisa's death certificate.

Uncle Ed believed his maternal grandparents were here by 1850 and the 1900 census would suggest he was correct. There George Becker, son of Henry and Louisa, says that he was born in Maryland and his birth date is June, 1850.

Louisa Becker shows up in the 1900 census also, as a widow living alone at 1234 Lexington Street, Baltimore. Unfortunately, the space following the question "Year emigrated to U.S." is blank. She states she is a naturalized citizen, but I have been unable to find naturalization records for her or for Henry at the Hall of Records in Annapolis. (Suspect further searching will turn up this vital information)

Other puzzling data on Louisa's 1900 census record:
    "Mother of how many children" Louisa says 10!
    "Number of children living" Louisa says 7
She also states she can speak English but "cannot read or write" (English? German? Both?) One wonders if she understood the questions about children. Ed and Lula knew of only 4 children of the marriage of Henry and Louisa. I think Louisa gave the number of her grandchildren as she DID have 7 living ones in 1900 and I know of two others who had previously died in infancy.

Lula (real name Louise and thus a namesake of Louisa Becker) told me that her maternal grandmother always seemed to her to be very stern. She remembered her living in a little house on Lexington St., said she had very erect carriage (posture), and that she always wore black. The photo I have of her bears out this description.

* I also checked the archives of the City of Baltimore

129

I checked the Baltimore directories to try to find Henry Becker. Here is what I found:

    1849-50 - no Henry Baecker or Baker who was a cabinet maker

    1853-54 Matchett's Baltimore Directory
        Baker - Henry - cabinetmaker, 49 Constitution (p. 22)
        Baker, Henry - cabinetmaker, 101 Franklin

    1856-57 - nine Henry Bakers listed but none cabinetmakers

    1858 Boyd's Baltimore City directory
        Baecker, Heinrich - furniture, 161 E. Fayette (p.33)
            Residence - same address

    1860   Baker, Henry - cabinetmaker, 161 E. Fayette (note Anglicized name)

    1864 - Baker, Henry - cabinetmaker, 159 E. Fayette

    1865-66 Ditto above

    1870 through 1875 - not listed

Here is some additional information on Henry and Louisa's children which fleshes out the plain facts on the family data sheet:

    Son George worked at one time for his brother-in-law Henry Sehrt at the latter's store. George and Gertrude had two daughters, Caroline (married name Andrews) and Emma (married name Miller).

    Son Herman was, according to Lula, the black sheep of the family. He was an alcoholic who ended up in Bay View, a home for indigent alcoholics.

    Daughter Caroline married Henry Sehrt and had 5 children, only three of whom lived to adulthood. More about them anon.

    Son Henry J. and his wife Eva, had Harry Walling and Bessie. Bessie died in 1895 at the age of 23 months, but Harry lived until 1964, dying at age 76. Henry J., I'm told, was the first to spell the family name in the English way, Baker (maybe not; see above). Henry worked for S. Kann & Sons, a department store on South Broadway in Baltimore, and was a pillar of Faith Reformed Church. He died at age 40 leaving Aunt Eva with a 14 year old son. Harry grew up to marry Margaret Eckhart, a friend of his cousin Lula, and I knew them as "Cousin Harry" and "Cousin Margaret". Their only child, Warren Baker, now lives in *Carmel,* CA with his second wife. He fathered a son, David, by his first wife, Martha Jane, and adopted two daughters with his second wife, Kelly. Warren is keenly interested in genealogy, so might be a good source. Eva Baker & Caroline Sehrt were very close friends as well as sisters-in-law.

In summary, Henry Baecker *probably* came to the US around 1849. He and his wife ,Louisa, both came from the Black Forest area of Germany. They had four children born in the USA and Henry supported them as a cabinetmaker. He died at aged 67 in 1890 and Louisa survived him for another 19 years. We know of some of their descendants today named Baker, Sperry, Parks, Markline, Cameron, Hendrickson, etc.

*Warren Baker died
22 April 1995 in Carmel,*

130

FAMILY GROUP NO. _____

Husband's Full Name Henry Baecker

This information Obtained From:	Husband's Data	Day Month Year	City, Town or Place	County or Province, etc.	State or Country	Add. Info. on Husband
Baltimore Cemetery	Birth	7 Nov 1822			Germany	
Death certificate.	Chr'nd					
1900 Census	Marr.					
Recollections of	Death	27 Aug 1890	Baltimore		Maryland	
Edward Sehrt and	Burial	Baltimore Cemetery, North Ave., Baltimore, MD				
Lula Cameron	Places of Residence					
	Occupation Cabinetmaker		Church Affiliation		Military Rec.	
	Other wives, if any. No. (1) (2) etc. Make separate sheet for each marr.					
	His Father		Baecker	Mother's Maiden Name		

Wife's Full Maiden Name Louisa

	Wife's Data	Day Month Year	City, Town or Place	County or Province, etc	State or Country	Add. Info. on Wife
	Birth	22 Aug 1822			Germany	
	Chr'nd					
	Death	17 May 1909	Baltimore		Maryland	
	Burial	Baltimore Cemetery, North Avenue, Balto., MD				
Compiler Loidah Cameron	Places of Residence					
Address	Occupation		Church Affiliation		Military Rec.	
City, State	Other husbands, if any. No. (1) (2) etc. Make separate sheet for each marr.					
Date March 1999	Her Father			Mother's Maiden Name		

Sex	Children's Names in Full (Arrange in order of birth)	Children's Data	Day Month Year	City, Town or Place	County or Province, etc.	State or Country	Add. info. on Children
	1 George	Birth	7 June 1850	Baltimore		MD	Daughters
		Marr.					Caroline t
	Full Name of Spouse	Death	8 Mar 1908	Baltimore		MD	Emma
	Gertrude	Burial	Baltimore Cemetery, North Ave., Baltimore		MD	
	2 Herman	Birth	15 Oct 1854	Baltimore		MD	
		Marr.					
	Full Name of Spouse	Death	9 April 1910				
		Burial	Baltimore Cemetery, North Ave. Baltimore, MD				
	3 Caroline	Birth	5 May 1858	Baltimore		MD	6
		Marr.					children
	Full Name of Spouse Henry Sehrt	Death	9 May 1928				
		Burial	Loudon Park Cemetery	Baltimore, MD		
	4 Henry J.	Birth	17 Aug 1863				One son Harry
		Marr.					Walling Bakers
	Full Name of Spouse Eva Walling	Death	8 Mar 1904				Infant daugh
		Burial	Loudon Park Cemetery	Baltimore, MD		ter died at
	5	Birth					23 months
		Marr.					
	Full Name of Spouse	Death					
		Burial					
	6	Birth					
		Marr.					
	Full Name of Spouse	Death					
		Burial					
	7	Birth					
		Marr.					
	Full Name of Spouse	Death					
		Burial					
	8	Birth					
		Marr.					
	Full Name of Spouse	Death					
		Burial					
	9	Birth					
		Marr.					
	Full Name of Spouse	Death					
		Burial					
	10	Birth					
		Marr.					
	Full Name of Spouse	Death					
		Burial					

* For additional children use Everton Publishers' Children Continuation Sheet, Form A11

Uncle Ed Chronicles

Sehrt, Edward

Faculty [edit]

Words spoken before man could write and those written before man could print have claimed the bondage of Dr. Edward Henry Sehrt for more than 30 years. It is a bondage which the bonded thoroughly enjoys. Dr. Sehrt, professor of German at the University since 1926, is noted in this country and abroad as an authority in Germanic and comparative philology because he has been an indefatigable researcher in the field since college days in nearby Baltimore.

As a young student of mathematics at Johns Hopkins University he chose an elective course in Sanskrit and followed this with Old English. At this point scholarship lost a mathematician and gained a linguist. Perhaps because Dr. Sehrt enjoyed his undergraduate work so much, he still looks forward each summer to teaching a course in first year German. He likes to see students "start with nothing and gradually build up ability to use a language." In fact Dr. Sehrt says regretfully he feels that something is missing those terms when he does not have a beginner's course.

Most of Dr. Sehrt's time is given to teaching and research in such subjects as Middle High German, Gothic, Old High German, Old Saxon, Old Norse, Comparative Germanic Grammar, Introduction to Linguistics, Indo-European Language, and Sanskrit. He will tell you with a twinkle in his eye that philologists have the poorest public relations of anyone because it is almost impossible to explain what they are doing to someone who is not doing the same thing. He says that delving into linguistics is in a way fascinating as the working of puzzles is fascinating. The outcome of the problem attacked, he says, has more meaning than the answers in a puzzle book. For Dr. Sehrt there are no "dead languages." He is convinced that study of "dead languages" is a live subject, that comparative linguistics contribute to modern culture and discovery as well as to the understanding of things past.

Among Dr. Sehrt's translations are those done for a professor of medical history, documents from the Old Testament period. Medical researchers often find clues to new discoveries in information about diseases prevalent hundreds of years ago.

Dr. Sehrt has been a word maker. He has helped the United States Weather Bureau compile a dictionary of meteorological terms which will best convey scientific concepts.

He points out that "the linguists can often give information of importance to the historian, the archeologist, the sociologist, the paleontologist, or the psychologist."

For years Dr. Sehrt has been publishing works of the monk Notker, tenth century teacher of St. Gall Monastery in Switzerland. In compiling a complete concordance of Notker's works, publishing his "Psalter" together with Latin commentaries, Dr. Sehrt has added to knowledge about the laws of language change - such as why and how consonants change, why words live and die and when.

Development of these laws permit scholars to reconstruct languages used as long ago as 3000 B.C., which is 1000 or more years before the written word appeared. Knowledge of what words were used then tells much about life before the written word. Dr. Sehrt points out that trends in thought, behavior, ideals, and customs of peoples of the world are traceable in language trends. "The Norman French after the Battle of Hastings almost changed English into a Romance language." At one time the French adopted many German words dealing with war, and the Germans in the 12th and 13th centuries used French words of chivalry. With apologies to a certain advertiser, Dr. Sehrt looks like "a scholar of distinction." His 22 years on the faculty at the University, always assigned to fourth floor offices, have kept this tall figure straight. His brisk manner belies the grey hairs, and the mischievous look that comes and goes as he talks denotes a love of company that makes one wonder how he can be a devotee of quiet study.

The answer must be that he possesses three qualities which he recommends for any linguistic scholar-some knowledge of mathematics, some understanding of psychology, and a special endowment of "Sitzfleisch." This descriptive German word is best translated "sitting flesh" although the dictionary calls it "assiduity." Dr. Sehrt is an admirer of the modern age despite the antiquity with which his research is concerned. Because of modern mechanical enterprise he has seen the study of linguistics shift from a closed corporation for European scholars to the American armchair.

Those who have always associated scholarly research with pale young men in cold old uncomfortable libraries are shamefully behind the times, according to Dr. Sehrt.

He shudders to recall his early research performed in freezing damp reading rooms in the British Museum and the Bibliotheque Nationale in Paris. Today he enjoys instead sitting in "my cozy chair beside a small desk and a three foot high pile of photostats and a foot high pile of microfilms. On the table is a projector, a brimming coffee pot, cup and saucer, and an ample supply of cigarettes and cigars."

[edit]

Document Information

Images: 0
Photographic Credit: n/a
Author or Source: *GWU Alumni Review*, December 1948
Document Location: University Archives
Date Added to Encyclopedia: December 21, 2006
Prepared by: Lyle Slovick

[edit]

For more information about GW history

Contact:

Special Collections Research Center [1]
The Melvin Gelman Library [2]
The George Washington University [3]
2130 H Street, NW Suite 704
Washington, DC 20052
202-994-7549
mailto:archives@gwu.edu
Please send us your questions and comments about the encyclopedia.
This site is maintained by the Special Collections Research Center and the Web Development Group.

Categories: People | Faculty | All Articles

Misc. Markline and Other Info

Markline Family Tree
From Philip Markline

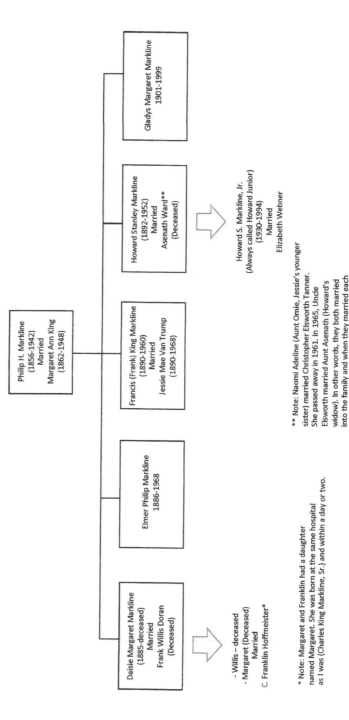

Philip H. Markline
(1856-1942)
Married
Margaret Ann King
(1862-1948)

Daisie Margaret Markline
(1885-deceased)
Married
Frank Willis Doran
(Deceased)

Elmer Philip Markline
1886-1968

Francis (Frank) King Markline
(1890-1960)
Married
Jessie Mae Van Trump
(1890-1968)

Howard Stanley Markline
(1892-1952)
Married
Asenath Ward**
(Deceased)

Gladys Margaret Markline
1901-1999

- Willis – deceased
- Margaret (Deceased)
  Married
  C. Franklin Hoffmeister*

Howard S. Markline, Jr.
(Always called Howard Junior)
(1930-1994)
Married
Elizabeth Webner

* Note: Margaret and Franklin had a daughter named Margaret. She was born at the same hospital as I was (Charles King Markline, Sr.) and within a day or two.

** Note: Naomi Adeline (Aunt Omie, Jessie's younger sister) married Christopher Elsworth Tanner. She passed away in 1961. In 1965, Uncle Elsworth married Aunt Asenath (Howard's widow). In other words, they both married into the family and when they married each other they married "Out" of the family. I don't make this stuff up.

Updated October 21, 2016

Markline Family Tree
From Francis (Frank) Markline

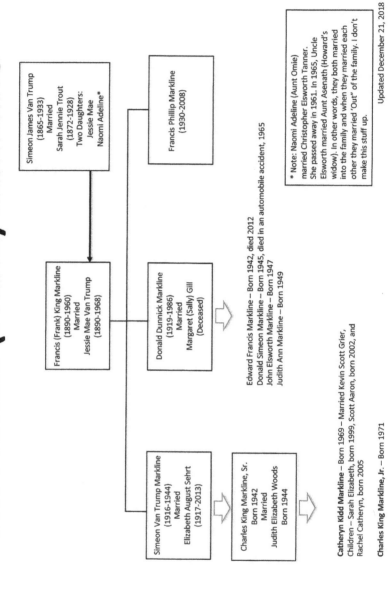

Simeon James Van Trump
(1865-1933)
Married
Sarah Jennie Trout
(1872-1928)
Two Daughters:
Jessie Mae
Naomi Adeline*

Francis Phillip Markline
(1930-2008)

Francis (Frank) King Markline
(1890-1960)
Married
Jessie Mae Van Trump
(1890-1968)

Donald Dunnick Markline
(1919-1986)
Married
Margaret (Sally) Gill
(Deceased)

Edward Francis Markline – Born 1942, died 2012
Donald Simeon Markline – Born 1945, died in an automobile accident, 1965
John Elsworth Markline – Born 1947
Judith Ann Markline – Born 1949

Simeon Van Trump Markline
(1916-1944)
Married
Elizabeth August Sehrt
(1917-2013)

Charles King Markline, Sr.
Born 1942
Married
Judith Elizabeth Woods
Born 1944

Catheryn Kidd Markline – Born 1969 – Married Kevin Scott Grier,
Children – Sarah Elizabeth, born 1999, Scott Aaron, born 2002, and
Rachel Catheryn, born 2005

Charles King Markline, Jr. – Born 1971

Updated December 21, 2018

* Note: Naomi Adeline (Aunt Omie) married Christopher Elsworth Tanner. She passed away in 1961. In 1965, Uncle Elsworth married Aunt Asenath (Howard's widow). In other words, they both married into the family and when they married each other they married 'Out' of the family. I don't make this stuff up.

John Jacob Markline

M. Elizabeth (1st wife who died in childbirth
             child buried with her.)
   Barbara (Springer) (second wife)
            No record of either wives maiden names.
   Children

John Nicholas
Married
Mary Feisler

   Children:

(1) Catherine (Katie)
    M. Henry Johnson
       Children:
          Mary   M. John DeMarco
          Evelyn   M. Howard Belt
          Howard   M. Ruth Shackelford
          Lena   M. Wayne Edwards
          Norman   M. Mary Lee Stanley
          Helen Mae M. Richard Houck

(2) William
    M. Emma Smith
       Children:
          Ross   M. Elmira Sutton

(3) Benjamin
    M. Mary Hildt
       Children:
          None

(4) John
    M. Edith Smith
       Children:
          Margaret   M. Edgar Harkins
          John   Single
          Doris   M. John Funkhouser
          Mary   M. Vernon Smith
          Benjamin   M. Dorothy

(6) George Adam
    M. Edith Wisotzkey
       Children:
          Richard   M. Mary Virginia Bailey

(5) Andrew
    M. Laura Runnan
       Children:
          Edward M. Lydia --
          Louis   M Hester --

143

Philip (Continued)
Elmer - single
Francis (Frank)
    M. Jessie VanTrump
    Children:
    Simeon M. Betty Sehrt
        Children:
            Charles King
            Donald M. Margaret (Sally)
                Gill
    Children:
        Edward
        Simeon (deceased)
        John
        Judith

Howard
    M. L. Asenath Ward
    Children:
        Howard S. Markline, Jr.
            M. Elizabeth Webner
    Gladys - single

Mary
    M. Philip King
    Children Lottie (Charlotte?)
        M. John Hunt
        Children:
            Homer M. Mary Neal
            Hilda M. Gilbert Royston
            Edna M. Elwood Jones
            Maurice M. Mary Ellen Dueer

        Grace M. Joseph Bayne
            No children

George
    M. Annie Willis
    Children
        Hugh M. Martha Lou --
        Lora M. ? Merritt
        Evelyn M. L.D. Edge
        Evelyn now deceased
        George M. Ruth --

(7) Louis
    M. Elma Greaser
    Children:
        Robert M. Jean --
        Edith M. Herbert Gilland
        Kenneth M. Marian Pittinger
        Eva Marie M. Donald W. Lolover
        Janice M. Russell Eckert
        George ?
        Patricia ?

(8) Helen
    M. Edwin Troyer
    Children:
        Dorothy M William Gemmill

Henry
    Single
    (was buried in wedding clothes before wedding)

Elizabeth
    Married
    Henry Croise
    No record of her or children

Philip:
    Married
    Margaret Ann King

    Children:
        Daisie
            M. Frank Willis Doran
            Children:
                Willis (single-deceased)
                Margaret
                    M. C. Franklin Hoffmaster

144

George Henry Markline M. Annie Tarrant Willis

Children:
(1) Evelyn M. L. D. Edge
    Child: L. D. Edge, Jr. (Buddy) M. Lorraine DeRoy
            Children: Lorraine
                       Patricia

(2) Lora Elizabeth M. Melton Tucker Merritt ("Boo")
    Child: Millicent Elizabeth M. Gerald Allen Howell ("Boots")
            Children: Mark Harold
                       David Tucker
                       Shawn Elizabeth
                       John

(3) Hugh Wallace M. Martha Lou Morton
    Child: Martha Ann M. Harry L. Hopkins
            Children: Peter Ashley
                       Heather Caroline

(4) George Henry, Jr. M. Eleanor Ruth Dubuisson
    Children: George Henry, III M. Cathy Taylor
               Children: George Henry, IV
                          Kenneth Lee

               Dorothy Denise M. Patrick Henry Jones (Later Divorced)
               Child: Jeffry Patrick

               Dorothy Denise also M. Robert Dengler

rootsweb *Finding our roots together.*

AN
ancestry.com
COMMUNITY

DISCOVER MORE >

| Home | Searches | Family Trees | Mailing Lists | Message Boards | Web Sites | Passwords | Help |

Search Hundreds of Thousands of Family Trees

First Name: [   ]   Last Name: [   ]   [Search]

OneGreatFamily

Families of Lancaster, Philadelphia & York County, PA

Entries: 11443   Updated: 2009-06-13 04:03:14 UTC (Sat)   Contact: Cheryl L   clginvb@cox.net

Index | Individual | Descendancy | Download GEDCOM | Public Profile

Descendant Register, Generation No. 1

→ 1. Simeon Oliver VAN TRUMP was born 19 JAN 1817, and died 12 MAR 1891. He was buried in West Liberty, MD. He married Elizabeth Ann WEBB 23 DEC 1858, daughter of Richard Jr. WEBB and Mary WALTON. She was born 18 OCT 1825 in Fawn Twp., York, PA, and died 19 JAN 1898. She was buried in Methodist Cemetery, West Liberty, Md..

Children of Simeon Oliver VAN TRUMP and Elizabeth Ann WEBB are:
  2   i. Robert VAN TRUMP was born 2 OCT 1859, and died 12 MAR 1862.
  + 3   ii. Samuel(?) VAN TRUMP was born 1 MAR 1862, and died 31 JUL 1929.
→ + 4   iii. Simeon James VAN TRUMP was born 12 OCT 1865, and died 22 APR 1933.

Descendant Register, Generation No. 2

3. Samuel(?) VAN TRUMP (Simeon Oliver VAN TRUMP[1]) was born 1 MAR 1862, and died 31 JUL 1929. He married Annie KIRKWOOD.

Child of Samuel(?) VAN TRUMP and Annie KIRKWOOD is:
  5   i. Garfield Sellman VAN TRUMP.

→ 4. Simeon James VAN TRUMP (Simeon Oliver VAN TRUMP[1]) was born 12 OCT 1865, and died 22 APR 1933. He was buried in West Liberty, MD. He married Sarah Jennie TROUT 4 SEP 1890. She was born 1872, and died 1928. She was buried in West Liberty, MD.
Naomi

Christopher
Ellsworth   Tanner

Children of Simeon James VAN TRUMP and Sarah Jennie TROUT are:
  6   i. Neomia Adeline VAN TRUMP died 3 APR 1961 in Baltimore, Md.. She married Ellsworth TENNER.
→ 7   ii. Jessie M. VAN TRUMP was born 1892, and died 15 MAY 1968.

May

Descendant Register, Generation No. 3

7. Jessie M. VAN TRUMP (Simeon James VAN TRUMP[2], Simeon Oliver VAN TRUMP[1]) was born 1892, and died 15 MAY

1968. She was buried in Vernons Cemetery, White Hall, Md.. She married Francis King MARKLINE ABT 1915.

Children of Jessie M. VAN TRUMP and Francis King MARKLINE are: Augusta Sehrt
→ 8   i. Dr Simeon Van Trump MARKLINE. He married Elizabeth Agusta SHUHART?.
  9   ii. Donald D. MARKLINE. — Dunnick
  10   iii. Francis C. MARKLINE.   Phillip

Index | Individual | Descendancy | Download GEDCOM | Public Profile

---

Printer Friendly Version Search Ancestry Search WorldConnect Join Ancestry.com Today!

WorldConnect Home | WorldConnect Global Search | WorldConnect Help

---

James

Simeon Van Trump, 1865 – 1933

Simeon Van Trump was born on month day 1865, to Samuel Oliver Van Trump and Elizabeth Ann Quigley (born Webb).

Samuel was born on January 19 1817.

Elizabeth was born on October 18 1825, in Fawn Twp, York Cty, PA.

Simeon had 4 siblings: Robert Van Trump and 3 other siblings.

Simeon married Sarah Jennie Van Trump (born Trout).

Sarah was born in 1872. *Naomi Tanner*

They had 2 daughters: Nevina Adeline Tanner (born Van Trump) and one other child.

Simeon passed away on month day 1933, at age 67 at death place, Maryland.

He was buried at burial place, Maryland.

Buried in Liberty Ind. West Cemetery

Documents of Simeon Van Trump

Simeon J Van Trump in 1910 United States Federal Census

Simeon J Van Trump was born circa 1866, at birth place, Maryland.

Simeon married Sarah J Van Trump.

They had 2 children: Jessie M Van Trump and one other child.

Simeon lived in 1910, at address, Maryland.

Jessie May = Grandmother maxlinne

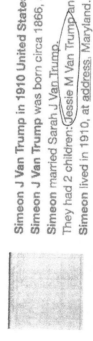

Simeon Vantrump in 1900 United States Federal Census

Simeon Vantrump was born in month 1865, at birth place, Maryland.

Simeon married Sarah J Vantrump circa 1891, at age 25.

They had 2 children: Naomi A Vantrump and one other child.

Simeon lived in 1900, at address, Maryland.

Simeon James Van Trump, 1865 - 1933

Simeon James Van Trump was born on month day 1865, at birth place, Maryland, to Simeon O Van Trump and Elizabeth Ann Webb.

Simeon had 5 siblings: Samuel S Van Trump, Robert Van Trump and 3 other siblings.

Simeon married Sarah Jennie Van Trump on month day 1890, at age 24 at marriage place, Maryland. They had 4 children: Jessie M Markline and 3 other children.

Simeon lived in 1910, at address, Maryland.

Simeon passed away on month day 1933, at age 67 at death place, Maryland.

Simeon O Van Trump, 1816 - 1891

Simeon O Van Trump was born on month day 1816, at birth place, Maryland.

Simeon married Elizabeth A. (___ Van Trump on month day 1856, at age 42  at marriage place, Maryland. They had 4 children: Simeon James Van Trump and 3 other children.

Simeon married Elizabeth Ann Webb on month day 1858, at age 42 at marriage place, Maryland.

Simeon lived in 1880, at address, Maryland.

He lived in 1860, at address, Maryland.

Simeon passed away on month day 1891, at age 74 at death place, Maryland.

149

Trump, a small cross- time for a woman presid
roads in Baltimore County, says.
about five miles from Penn-
sylvania, was named after a 19th-century settler
named Simeon O. Van Trump, who ran a grocery store
on Old York Road near West Liberty Road. Today few
remember the Trump name, though it is still a
neighborhood labeled on street maps. The farming
community retains many descendants from the
families of Van Trump's day, and their names can be
found on street signs and on the gravestones behind
the 228-year old West Liberty United Methodist
Church. The West Liberty neighborhood, as Trump is
now known, is part of White Hall.

Margaret Ann Markline (born King), 1862 - 1948

Margaret Ann Markline was born in <u>month</u> 1862, at <u>birth place</u>, Maryland, to Michael King and Catherine E. King.

Margaret had 6 siblings: Katherine E. King, Frederic King and <u>4 other siblings</u>.

Margaret married Philip H Markline circa 1884, at age 21 at <u>marriage place</u>, Maryland.

They had one son: Francis King Markline. — *Two doughters*

Margaret lived in 1900, at <u>address</u>, Maryland. *Three Sons*

She lived in 1920, at <u>address</u>, Maryland.

She lived in 1930, at <u>address</u>, Maryland.

She lived in 1935, at <u>address</u>.

She lived in 1940, at <u>address</u>, Maryland.

Margaret passed away in 1948, at age 85 at <u>death place</u>, Maryland.

1998—Former home of Philip Markline
White hall, just above the Vernon cemetety
Building on the right was the funeral home

The Band

Simeon Markline	*Company Commander*
Allen Dudley	*Second-in-Command*
Carl Bollinger	*First Lieutenant*
Frank Brown	*First Sergeant*
Herman Williams	*Sergeant*
George Skinner	*Sergeant*
Charles Ehrhardt	*Corporal*
John Elliot	*Corporal*
John Lavin	*Corporal*
Frank Malone	*Corporal*

Eugene Cronin	Raymond Buchman
Kirk Fallin	Warren Moore
Lewis Gordon	Joseph Myers
Walter Hoke	John Potter
William Hood	Norman Rausch
Irving Jackson	James Stoner
Howard Sullivan	Marshall Wilson
August Brust	

ADDITIONAL MEMBERS

Harold Biehl	Aubrey Schneider
John Elseroad	Wayne Strasbaugh
Walter Mullinix	Sterling Zimmerman

Harry Griggs

SIMEON MARKLINE	*Captain*
MISS BETTY SEHRT	*Sponsor*
ALLEN DUDLEY	*Second-in-Command*

SIMEON VAN TRUMP MARKLINE

*DELTA PI ALPHA; College Orchestra, 1, 2, 3, 4;
Band, 1, 2, 3, 4; Y. M. C. A., 1, 2; Sunday School,
2, 3, 4; Officers' Club; R. O. T. C. Captain, Band;
Intra-Mural Athletics, 1, 2, 3, 4.*

"Mark" . . . straightforward, blunt, and buoyant
. . . a trumpeter . . . practical joker . . . likes to argue
. . . often seen at a corner table in the "Grill" . . .
chief objects of conversation—baseball and love.

UNiversity 8557, Res. HO. 0931   Reg. No. 3890

SIMEON V. T. MARKLINE, M. D.

900 W. 37th Street,   BALTIMORE, MARYLAND

Office Hours: 9 to 10 A. M., 6:30 to 8:30 P. M. and by Appointment

Patient's
Name...

Address..Date...........................

℞ to navy,
I am not going to
marry you.

Love
Charles

....M. D.

Non-Repetatur unless directed.

155

CERTIFICATE OF COPYRIGHT REGISTRATION

FORM TX

This certificate, issued under the seal of the Copyright Office in accordance with the provisions of section 410(a) of title 17, United States Code, attests that copyright registration has been made for the work identified below. The information in this certificate has been made a part of the Copyright Office records.

David L. Ladd

REGISTER OF COPYRIGHTS
United States of America

80-16,490

REGISTRATION NUMBER
TX (TX) 557-522 TXU

EFFECTIVE DATE OF REGISTRATION
SEP 15 1980
(Month)   (Day)   (Year)

DO NOT WRITE ABOVE THIS LINE. IF YOU NEED MORE SPACE, USE CONTINUATION SHEET (FORM TX/CON)

(1) Title

TITLE OF THIS WORK: A COMPARATIVE ANALYSIS OF COLLEGE ENTRY PROGRAM AND HIGH SCHOOL INITIAL STUDENTS: STUDY HABITS AND ATTITUDES, SEX, AGE, GPAS, AND OTHER SELECTED VARIABLES

PREVIOUS OR ALTERNATIVE TITLES:

If a periodical or serial give: Vol....... No....... Issue Date......................

PUBLICATION AS A CONTRIBUTION: (If this work was published as a contribution to a periodical, serial, or collection, give information about the collective work in which the contribution appeared.)

Title of Collective Work: .... Vol....... No..... Date .... Pages............

(2) Author(s)

IMPORTANT: Under the law, the "author" of a "work made for hire" is generally the employer, not the employee (see instructions). If any part of this work was "made for hire" check "Yes" in the space provided, give the employer (or other person for whom the work was prepared) as "Author" of that part, and leave the space for dates blank.

1
NAME OF AUTHOR: CHARLES KING MARKLINE
Was this author's contribution to the work a "work made for hire"? Yes...... No. X...
DATES OF BIRTH AND DEATH: Born 1942. Died .... (Year) (Year)
AUTHOR'S NATIONALITY OR DOMICILE: Citizen of USA or Domiciled in ......
WAS THIS AUTHOR'S CONTRIBUTION TO THE WORK: Anonymous? Yes...... No. X. Pseudonymous? Yes...... No. X.
If the answer to either of these questions is "Yes," see detailed instructions attached.
AUTHOR OF: (Briefly describe nature of this author's contribution) ENTIRE TEXT

2
NAME OF AUTHOR:
Was this author's contribution to the work a "work made for hire"? Yes...... No......
DATES OF BIRTH AND DEATH: Born .... Died .... (Year) (Year)
AUTHOR'S NATIONALITY OR DOMICILE: Citizen of ...... or Domiciled in ......
WAS THIS AUTHOR'S CONTRIBUTION TO THE WORK: Anonymous? Yes...... No...... Pseudonymous? Yes...... No......
If the answer to either of these questions is "Yes," see detailed instructions attached.
AUTHOR OF: (Briefly describe nature of this author's contribution)

3
NAME OF AUTHOR:
Was this author's contribution to the work a "work made for hire"? Yes...... No......
DATES OF BIRTH AND DEATH: Born .... Died .... (Year) (Year)
AUTHOR'S NATIONALITY OR DOMICILE: Citizen of ...... or Domiciled in ......
WAS THIS AUTHOR'S CONTRIBUTION TO THE WORK: Anonymous? Yes...... No...... Pseudonymous? Yes...... No......
If the answer to either of these questions is "Yes," see detailed instructions attached.
AUTHOR OF: (Briefly describe nature of this author's contribution)

(3) Creation and Publication

YEAR IN WHICH CREATION OF THIS WORK WAS COMPLETED: Year 1980
(This information must be given in all cases.)

DATE AND NATION OF FIRST PUBLICATION: Date AUGUST 15, 1980 *
(Month) (Day) (Year)
Nation U.S.A. (Name of Country)
(Complete this block ONLY if this work has been published.)

(4) Claimant(s)

NAME(S) AND ADDRESS(ES) OF COPYRIGHT CLAIMANT(S):
CHARLES KING MARKLINE
120 GEMINI
LOMPOC, CA 93436

TRANSFER: (If the copyright claimant(s) named here in space 4 are different from the author(s) named in space 2, give a brief statement of how the claimant(s) obtained ownership of the copyright.)

---

* Complete all applicable spaces (numbers 5-11) on the reverse side of this page
* Follow detailed instructions attached • Sign the form at line 10

DO NOT WRITE HERE

TX · 557-522

DO NOT WRITE ABOVE THIS LINE. IF YOU NEED ADDITIONAL SPACE, USE CONTINUATION SHEET (FORM TX/CON)

PREVIOUS REGISTRATION:

- Has registration for this work. or for an earlier version of this work, already been made in the Copyright Office?   Yes........ No X ......
- If your answer is "Yes," why is another registration being sought? (Check appropriate box)
  - ☐ This is the first published edition of a work previously registered in unpublished form.
  - ☐ This is the first application submitted by this author as copyright claimant.
  - ☐ This is a changed version of the work, as shown by line 6 of this application.
- If your answer is "Yes," give: Previous Registration Number .... Year of Registration ....

(5) Previ ...
Registra
tion

COMPILATION OR DERIVATIVE WORK: (See instructions)

PREEXISTING MATERIAL: (Identify any preexisting work or works that this work is based on or incorporates.)

{ ....

MATERIAL ADDED TO THIS WORK: (Give a brief, general statement of the material that has been added to this work and in which copyright is claimed.)

{ ....

(6) Comp.
o.
Derivative
Wor

MANUFACTURERS AND LOCATIONS: (If this is a published work consisting preponderantly of nondramatic literary material in English, the law may require that the copies be manufactured in the United States or Canada for full protection. If so, the names of the manufacturers who performed certain processes, and the places where these processes were performed *must* be given. See instructions for details.)

NAMES OF MANUFACTURERS	PLACES OF MANUFACTURE
UNIVERSITY MICROFILMS INTERNATIONAL	ANN ARBOR, MICHIGAN 48106

(7) Manufactur
ing

REPRODUCTION FOR USE OF BLIND OR PHYSICALLY-HANDICAPPED PERSONS: (See instructions)

- Signature of this form at space 10, and a check in one of the boxes here in space 8, constitutes a non-exclusive grant of permission to the Library of Congress to reproduce and distribute solely for the blind and physically handicapped and under the conditions and limitations prescribed by the regulations of the Copyright Office: (1) copies of the work identified in space 1 of this application in Braille (or similar tactile symbols); or (2) phonorecords embodying a fixation of a reading of that work; or (3) both.

a ☒ Copies and phonorecords   b ☐ Copies Only   c ☐ Phonorecords Only

(8) License
For
Handica

DEPOSIT ACCOUNT: (If the registration fee is to be charged to a Deposit Account established in the Copyright Office, give name and number of Account.)

Name UNIVERSITY MICROFILMS INTERNATIONAL
Account Number 313130

CORRESPONDENCE: (Give name and address to which correspondence about this application should be sent.)
Name: UNIVERSITY MICROFILMS INTERNATIONAL
Address: 300 N. ZEEB RD.
ANN ARBOR,   MICHIGAN   48106
(City)   (State)   (ZIP)   (Apt.)

(9) Fee a
Correspo
ence

CERTIFICATION: ✱ I, the undersigned, hereby certify that I am the: (Check one)
☐ author ☐ other copyright claimant ☐ owner of exclusive right(s) ☒ authorized agent of: CHARLES KING MARKLINE
(Name of author or other copyright claimant, or owner of exclusive right(s))
of the work identified in this application and that the statements made by me in this application are correct to the best of my knowledge.

Handwritten signature: (X) *Doris Mann*
Typed or printed name..... DORIS MANN   Date AUG 2 0 1980

(10) Certificati
(Applica
must a
signer

CHARLES KING MARKLINE
(Name)
120 GEMINI
(Number, Street and Apartment Number)
LOMPOC, CA 93436
(City)   (State)   (ZIP code)

MAIL CERTIFICATE TO

(Certificate will be mailed in window envelope)

(11) Address
For Ret
of
Certifica

✱ 17 U.S.C. § 506(e): Any person who knowingly makes a false representation of a material fact in the application for copyright registration provided for by section 409, or in any written statement filed in connection with the application, shall be fined not more than $2,500.

☆U.S. GOVERNMENT PRINTING OFFICE: 1979-281-421/4

Mar. 1978-2

Port Deposit, Md.
Dec 1, 1959

Dear Betty,

We were shocked
to learn of the great sorrow
that has come to you. We
knew nothing of it until
I glanced through the
obituary Monday evening
on my return from
school. Had I known I
would have called at
the mortuary. I did not
even know she had been
under the doctor's care.
She was always so peppy
and cheerful that I even
now find it difficult to

believe she could have gone so quickly.

Betty, you girls have lost a wonderful mother and friend. Her one desire always seemed to be to make you both happy. I know you will miss her more and more as you think of pleasures you have shared. Keeping busy with your family and those who still need you is a wonderful panacea. You just must display a cheerful countenance for their sake, especially as the Christmas season draws nearer.

We are so sorry to miss. seeing Charles. His Grandpa is so very ill and suffers so horribly

Letter from grandmother Markline to mother
(RE: Mom Maw's death)

New Officers Appointed For Campus AFROTC

A new AFROTC staff, headed by Cadet Col. Charles K. Markline, is taking command of the division this fall.

Assisting Markline is Cadet Col. Stephen E. Harrison, vice division commander. Nine cadet officers make up the staff.

They are cadet lieutenant colonels Richard A. DeVoss (Operations,) Carville D. Duncan, (administration), Robert H. Emerson (material), Stephen H. Miller (comptroller), Harold H. Mills (Personnel) and C. Edmund Quarles (inspector).

Cadet Maj. Joseph M. Ferrante (personnel services) and cadet captains Andrew D. Faith (information), Harry F. Grant (demerit control), and James H. Williams (administrative assistant) make up the remainder.

Cadet lieutenant colonels Gary L. Curtin and Philip A. Hickok have been appointed to command the first and second wings respectively. Commanding the division's six groups are cadet lieutenant colonels Thomas E. Symonds and K. Max Perry and cadet majors Wasyl Kurinij, Charles E. Soellers, Knute A. Anderson, and John H. Harling.

Cadet Maj. Samuel A. Griffith and Cadet Capt. Rix M. Mills head the Cadet Leadership Academy.

Cadet Colonel—University of Meryland
AFROTC
1964

CARLTON R. SICKLES
MEMBER AT LARGE, MARYLAND

Congress of the United States
House of Representatives
Washington, D. C.

February 26, 1965

Mr. Charles Markline
Sigma Chi Fraternity House
College Park, Maryland

Dear Mr. Markline,

Congratulations on being named to

Who's Who in American Colleges and ✓

Universities. This is an honor of

great distinction.

May I take this opportunity to wish

you continued success in all of your

endeavors.

Very sincerely,

Carlton R. Sickles, M.C.

CRS/za

MARYLAND STATE DEPARTMENT OF HEALTH
DIVISION OF VITAL RECORDS, 301 W. PRESTON STREET, BALTIMORE, MARYLAND 21201

CERTIFICATE OF DEATH

1 DECEASED NAME (Type or print)	Jessie Van Trump Markline / *Jessie V.T. MARKLINE*		2a DATE OF DEATH May 15 1968	2b HOUR 6:5 M
3 SEX F	4 RACE W		5 DATE OF BIRTH Sept. 14, 1891	6 AGE (in years, last birthday) 76 YRS. IF UNDER 1 YEAR / IF UNDER 24 hrs

7c BIRTHPLACE (State or foreign country) Maryland	7b CITIZEN OF WHAT COUNTRY? U.S.A.	8 MARRIED ☐ NEVER MARRIED ☐ WIDOWED ☒ DIVORCED ☐	9 COUNTY OF DEATH Harford	Md.

10 CITY OR TOWN OF DEATH Havre de Grace	11 NAME OF HOSPITAL OR INSTITUTION (If not in hospital give street address) Harford Memorial		12a USUAL OCCUPATION (Kind of work done during most of working life, even if retired) school teacher	12b KIND OF BUSINESS OR INDUSTRY Education
13a USUAL RESIDENCE (Where deceased lived, if institution: Residence before admission) STATE Md	13b COUNTY Cecil	13c CITY OR TOWN Port Deposit	13d INSIDE CITY LIMITS? YES ☐ NO ☒	13e STREET AND NUMBER Colora Road RH

14 FATHER'S NAME First Simeon Middle J. Last Van Trump	15 MOTHER'S MAIDEN NAME First Jennie Middle Last Trout

15a WAS DECEASED EVER IN U.S. ARMED FORCES? (Yes, no, or unknown) No	16b SOCIAL SECURITY NO. 212-38-2315	17 INFORMANT Donald D. Markline	Address Parkton, Md. 21120

18. CAUSE OF DEATH (Enter only one cause per line for (a), (b), and (c).)

		APPROXIMATE INTERVAL BETWEEN ONSET AND DEATH
PART I. DEATH WAS CAUSED BY: IMMEDIATE CAUSE (a)	Hepatic failure	3 days
Conditions, if any, which gave rise to immediate cause (a), stating the underlying cause last. DUE TO, OR AS A CONSEQUENCE OF (b)	Carcinoma of Gall Bladder	?
DUE TO, OR AS A CONSEQUENCE OF (c)		

PART 2. OTHER SIGNIFICANT CONDITIONS CONTRIBUTING TO DEATH BUT NOT RELATED TO THE TERMINAL DISEASE OR CONDITION GIVEN IN PART 1(a)
ASCVD

19a DATE OF OPERATION 5/16/68	19b CONDITION FOR WHICH OPERATION WAS PERFORMED Jaundice	20a AUTOPSY? YES ☐ NO ☒	20b IF YES, WERE FINDINGS CONSIDERED IN CERTIFYING CAUSES OF DEATH?
21a ACCIDENT WAS UNDERLYING ☐ OR CONTRIBUTING ☐ CAUSE OF DEATH (If either, notify medical examiner)	21b TIME OF INJURY HOUR A.M. Month Day Year P.M. 19	21c HOW INJURY OCCURRED (Enter nature of injury in Part 1 or Part 2, Item 18.)	
21d INJURY OCCURRED While ☐ Not while ☐ at work at work	21e PLACE OF INJURY (AT HOME, FARM, STREET, FACTORY, OFFICE BUILDING, ETC.)	21f LOCATION Street or R.F.D. No. City or Town County State	

22a. I certify that (I) (this hospital) attended the deceased from 2/9, 1968, to 5/15, 1968, that (I) (we) last saw the deceased alive on 5/15/68 19___, and that in (my) (our) opinion death occurred on the date and hour and from the causes stated above, (I) (we) (did) (did not) view the body after death.

22b. SIGNATURE *A.W. Grigoleit MD*	DEGREE	ATTENDING PHYS. ☒	MED. DIRECTOR ☐	STAFF PHYS. ☐	22c. DATE SIGNED 5/15/68
22d. PHYSICIAN'S NAME (Type) A.W. GRIGOLEIT		22e. ADDRESS Havre de Grace			

23a. BURIAL, CREMATION, REMOVAL (Specify) Burial	23b. DATE 5/18/1968	23c. NAME OF CEMETERY OR CREMATORY Vernon	23d. LOCATION (City or Town) (County) (State) White Hall, Balto. Md.
24. FUNERAL DIRECTOR Charles E. Kurtz	ADDRESS Jarrettsville, Md	25a. REC'D BY REGISTRAR DATE MAY 17 1968	25b. REGISTRAR'S SIGNATURE *Charles Judge*

162

A P P R A I S A L

OF A

PORTION OF THE ESTATE OF

JESSIE MARKLINE

PROPERTY DATA:
This property consists of 112.9 acres of land located on Route 269 in the 7th election district of Cecil County, near the Town of Port Deposit.

The land is rolling and is located in the better dairy section of the county, and is zoned A.R. and F.R.

IMPROVEMENTS:

       The improvements on the farm, are listed on the assessment sheet, and is further shown on a layout of the farm buildings, as they existed.

THIS IS WHAT REMAINS OF THE BARN COMPLEX.

THESE BUILDINGS UNTOUCHED BY
FIRE, ARE N. OF THE HOUSE.

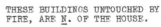

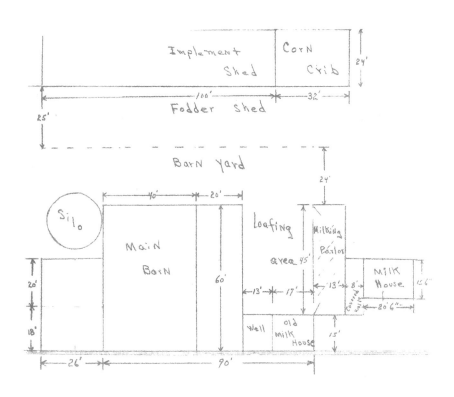

ASSESSMENTS:

Title reference R.R.C. 29 folio 31.

			BEFORE FIRE	AFTER FIRE
2	Ac.	homesite	$ 1,400.00	
86	"	tillable	10,320.00	
4	"	pasture	200.00	ditto
20	"	woodland	700.00	
.9	"	other	10.00	
Dwelling			$9,300.00	$ 2,500.00
Barn			2,500.00	
Harness shed			50.00	50.00
Other			100.00	100.00
Poultry house			100.00	100.00
Milk house			150.00	
Implement shed			300.00	
Corn crib			200.00	
Silo			400.00	400.00
Milking parlor			1,200.00	
Other milk house			150.00	150.00
TOTAL			$27,080.00	$15,930.00

Current tax rate 1970 - 1971

County	$2.72
State	.18
Total	$2.90

167

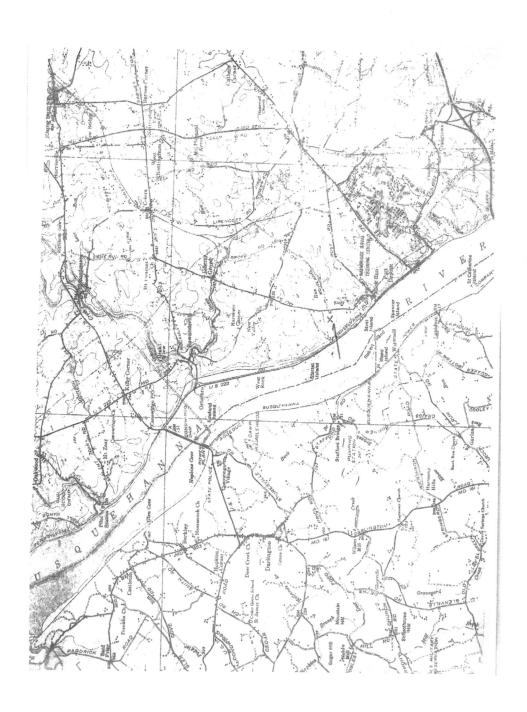

COST APPROACH TO VALUE:

                    In estimating the value of the farm buildings destroyed by fire, I have refered to local farm construction costs, have adjusted to the time of the fire, and have considered accrued depreciation, physical deterioration, and functional and economic obsolescence.

Main barn	2400 sq. ft.	¢ 16.50	$ 39,600.00
Loafing shed	1200 " "	5.00	6,000.00
Corn crib	768 " "	2.50	1,920.00
Implement shed	2400 " "	1.50	3,600.00
Old milk house	318 " "	3.00	954.00
Milking parlor	(4 cows)	1,400.00	5,600.00
Storage building	988 sq. ft.	11.00	10,868.00
			68,542.00
Less depreciation of 55%			37,698.00
Total estimated value			$ 30,844.00

169

COMPARABLE SALES:

        From Clyde Farmer to J. Brinsfield

        June 1966

        $ 55,000.00

        W.A.S. 193 folio 21

        From Floyd Kitner to Harold Montgomery

        October 1967

        $ 50,000.00

        W.A.S. 216 folio 640

        From Floyd Kitner to Montgomery Brothers

        October 1967

        $ 35,000.00

        W.A.S. 216 folio 633

        Edgar T. Marshall to John Killy Jr.

        January 1965

        $ 60,000.00

        W.A.S. 164 folio 540

In comparing the sales of the above properties, a grid system
was prepared to show all buildings by type, acreage of tillable
land, woodland, pasture, and other lands. Based on this information each sale was adjusted to April '69, and it was concluded
that this property was worth $ 70,000.00

SUMMARY:

By cost approach, the estimated value of the destroyed farm buildings was $30,844.00, and by comparable sales the over-all farm value was $70,000.00. This latter figure is more or less confirmed by a statement made September 9th, 1969 by Mr. Raymond G. Mueller, Extension Agent for Cecil County, who said," you folks are well aware of the trends in Cecil County. I expect the average figure for Maryland of $611.00 per acre in 1969 is actually low for Cecil County," hence 112.9 Acres at $611.00 equals $68,981.00.

This farm was operative, and in 1965 had an accredited T.B. free herd, which meant that the buildings had to conform to health department requirements, which confirms a good condition of buildings, that I estimate to have been worth $ 30,000.00

I hereby certify that I have personally examined this property and to the best of my knowledge and belief, the data on which this appraisal was made is true and correct; that no pertinent information has been overlooked, and that I have no interest, either present or contemplated in the property appraised or in any proceeds to be derived therefrom.

No responsibility is assumed by this Appraiser for matters which are of a legal nature, nor is any opinion on the title rendered herewith; good title is assumed.

This appraisal has been made in conformity with the highest professional standards of the National Association of Real Estate Appraisers.

George W. Lutz, Realtor - Appraiser

Homily: Charles Sperry
~~Text: John 14~~
Date: May 9, 2006
Location: Timonium
Preacher: Patti Collett

I want you to know that there is really nothing that I can say to you today that will make this any easier for you. The loss of a spouse of 54 years is an overwhelming loss. And the loss of a father with whom you had a nearly mystical relationship, you just can't replace that with words of any kind. So I'm not here to take away your sad feelings. What we're doing here today is acknowledging the gift that Charles has been to his family and friends, and we're here to thank God for this gift. And we're also here to remember a little and to say goodbye.

Charles was 93 years old. He is leaving behind his beloved wife, Betty, three children Wayne, Beth and Charles, two living brothers Harold and Russell, and 2 grandchildren and 3 great-grandchildren.

You have told me that Charles was a wonderful man, who loved his family very much, and who was loved very much in return. He was a man who could cause a lot of fun to happen around him, but a man who kept his emotions to himself except for that "pretty" smile that never left him. His 43 years as an employee of the C & P Telephone Co. speaks to his loyalty and his dedication to taking care of his family. He enjoyed sports, especially the Colts and Orioles, and playing golf with his three buddies who have preceded him to the best golf course ever. I'm told that one of his buddies has no doubt already greeted him with a hearty, "Charlie, what took you so long?"

We were talking a little on Sunday about the sadder side of a long life. With every year of life, there is also a year of struggles and pain. Jobs are lost, health declines, friends and loved ones go on to meet the Lord ahead of us. But struggles taken into account, we know in our hearts that we really can't complain about it when God graces us with nearly a century of life. There are so many gifts that we receive in a long life. The younger members of the family get the privilege of knowing their older family members and learning from them. The older family member gets to see the little ones mature and learn and graduate from schools and get awards and marry and have kids and get jobs, and through the younger ones, the older person gets to relive all these wonders of life. And everyone has the comfort of generous numbers of years of family traditions and the feeling of belonging to something bigger and more important than self.

I want you all to remember something today. Your relationship with Charles has not ended. It has changed, but it has not ended. This is what Jesus was trying to tell his disciples when he told them he was going on to another place and they knew the way to where he was going. Jesus was going on to a closer relationship with God than he could have in this mortal body. And we, as Christian believers know this, and we know where Charles is and we know the way. The way is to stay close to Jesus because he will guide us home as he has guided Charles home.

You can't make the feelings go away, but you can find peace. The peace that comes with living in God's time and not our own. The peace that comes with knowing, with certainty, that we' will be with our loved ones again. Listen one more time to these words of Jesus, spoken this time to you: **Peace, I leave with you. My peace I give to you. I do not give as the world gives. Do not let your hearts be troubled. Neither let them be afraid.**

About the Author

Charles King Markline, Sr., Ph.D. (Charlie)

He was born on the night of the first blackout in Baltimore during WWII. From the ages two to nine, Charlie and his mother lived with his maternal grandparents, an era in which children were expected to be seen and not heard. As a result, Charlie grew up observant, reserved, and a little shy. Later in his life, one year of military prep school cured his shyness.

Professionally, Charlie has been a man for all seasons. He is a retired officer from the United States Air Force, a former college professor, a Certified Professional Consultant to Management (CPCM), a former high school principal, a proposal manager for both Lockheed Martin and ASRC Federal, and now a published author.

His articles on communication, productivity, organizational management, and leadership have been published in the *Training* magazine, the *Texas Insurance Journal*, and *The Lakewood Report*.

Academically, Charlie earned a Bachelor of Science from the University of Maryland, an MBA from the University of North Dakota, and a Ph.D. from the United States International University.

He is a member of the Young America's Foundation President's Club, a group taking a lead role in preserving the Reagan Ranch, Rancho del Cielo.

Both of his children and the grandchildren are in California. Charlie and his wife, Judy, reside in the "Middle Kingdom," the central coast of California.

CPSIA information can be obtained
at www.ICGtesting.com
Printed in the USA
LVHW070508020621
689027LV00021B/2196